Nietzsche and Theology

Nietzsche and Theology

Craig Hovey

t&t clark

Published by T&T Clark

A Continuum imprint

The Tower Building, 11 York Road, London SE1 7NX

80 Maiden Lane, Suite 704, New York, NY 10038

www.continuumbooks.com

British Library Cataloguing-in-Publication Data

A catalogue record for this book is available from the British Library

ISBN-10: HB: 0-567-03151-9
          PB: 0-567-03152-7
ISBN-13: HB: 978-0-567-03151-8
          PB: 978-0-567-03152-5

Typeset by Newgen Imaging Systems Pvt Ltd, Chennai, India

Printed on acid-free paper in Great Britain by MPG Books Ltd, Bodmin, Cornwall

Contents

Preface

Living with Nietzsche for any length of time can be frightening and fruitful, and sometimes both simultaneously. I was reading Nietzsche and writing this book while teaching religion and ethics to seminarians and undergraduates, often searching for ways to share some of this material with my students. But I have also been particularly attentive to how living with Nietzsche might have an effect on other parts of my life—the non-academic parts—and how my view of Nietzsche and my reading of him might be affected by my friendships, the lengths of the walks I take, and the joys and sometimes tediousness of domestic life. This is all quite uninteresting to report except for the fact that I am persuaded Nietzsche would have approved and, more importantly, would have understood that this is actually nothing less than a philosophical life.

Nietzsche famously extolled the active life of strength, the independent vivacity of the unfettered mind. Yet the fact that he was, for periods of his own life, so dependent on the care of others surely indicates a kind of incongruity. His frequent three-day migraines would lift to a sudden flood of activity, innumerable eulogies to a very elusive toughness. But if he was sometimes dependent on others, compromising the self-reliant ideal in some respects, he still never had to care for a child. That nearly all of the words in the present book were written on one side or the other of the active care for my one-year-old son is not an incidental fact, nor can it be a source of pride. However, I have found it to be decisive and I am convinced that Nietzsche would have grasped its significance for the argument that it is.

This book's existence owes a great deal to the support of innumerable friends and colleagues. I am grateful to Jonathan Tran, Hien Huynh, Dan Vaca, and Justin Ashworth for thinking and reading with Nietzsche and with me. My parents and in-laws often provided time for me to write. The Benedictine Monks at St. Andrews Abbey in Valyermo, California, the Guest Center at Fuller Theological Seminary, and the staff at First Baptist Church of Redlands, California provided spaces.

Abbreviations

References to Nietzsche's works in English translation will follow the abbreviations listed below unless otherwise specified. It has become customary to make reference to the section numbers Nietzsche used in those works where they exist. In *Thus Spoke Zarathustra* and similarly structured works, I will refer to the book number followed by the name of the section.

A   *The Antichrist* 1888. Translated by Walter Kaufmann. In *The Portable Nietzsche*, edited and translated by Walter Kaufmann. London: Viking Penguin, 1968.

BGE   *Beyond Good and Evil* 1886. Translated by R. J. Hollingdale. London: Penguin, 1990.

BT   *The Birth of Tragedy* 1872. Translated by Francis Golffing. Garden City, NY: Doubleday, 1956.

D   *Daybreak* 1881. Translated by R. J. Hollingdale. Cambridge: Cambridge University Press, 2005.

EH   *Ecce Homo* 1888. Translated by R. J. Hollingdale. London: Penguin, 2004.

GM   *On the Genealogy of Morality* 1887. Translated by Carol Diethe. Cambridge: Cambridge University Press, 2004.

GS   *The Gay Science* 1882, 1887. Translated by Josefine Nauckhoff. Cambridge: Cambridge University Press, 2004.

HH   *Human, All Too Human* 1878. Translated by R. J. Hollingdale. Cambridge: Cambridge University Press, 2004.

NCW   *Nietzsche Contra Wagner* 1888. In *The Portable Nietzsche*. Edited and translated by Walter Kaufmann. London: Viking Penguin, 1968.

PT   *Philosophy and Truth: Selections from Nietzsche's Notebooks of the Early 1870's*. Edited and Translated by D. Breazeale. Amherst New York: Humanity Books, 1999.

Abbreviations

SL   *Selected Letters of Friedrich Nietzsche.* Edited and translated by Christopher Middleton. Cambridge: Hackett, 1996.

TI   *Twilight of the Idols or, How One Philosophizes with a Hammer* 1888. In *The Portable Nietzsche.* Edited and translated by Walter Kaufmann. London: Viking Penguin, 1968.

TL   "From: 'On Truth and Lie in an Extra-moral Sense'." In *The Portable Nietzsche.* Edited and translated by Walter Kaufmann. London: Viking Penguin, 1968.

UM   *Untimely Meditations* 1873–1876. Translated by R. J. Hollingdale. Cambridge: Cambridge University Press, 2004.

WP   *The Will to Power.* Translated by Walter Kaufmann and R. J. Hollingdale. New York: Vintage, 1968.

Z   *Thus Spoke Zarathustra* 1883–1885. Translated by Walter Kaufmann. In *The Portable Nietzsche.* Edited and translated by Walter Kaufmann. London: Viking Penguin, 1968.

Introduction

Should Christians even read Nietzsche? This is neither an idle question nor one with an obvious answer. Nietzsche captures the imagination and disarms the intellect, making potentially virulent this self-described Antichrist for Christian readers. The great Jesuit scholar, Frederick Copleston, found himself under pressure to include strong condemnations of Nietzsche when the first edition of his *Friedrich Nietzsche: Philosopher of Culture* was published in 1942. Nearly 30 years later, in the book's second edition, Copleston disclosed that he had bowed to ecclesiastical censorship and regretted the fact that his earlier denunciations continued to be reprinted. What had he said? I suspect he had in mind his earlier comments of this sort:

> [Nietzsche] claimed to be wicked, and he was correct—he *was* wicked. His campaign against Christianity and universal morality bear witness to the fact: in the latter respect he falls far short of a great pagan philosopher like Plato, who insisted on the absolute and universal character of moral values.[1]

Not only was Nietzsche a pagan but he also failed to be a virtuous pagan: his critiques of Christianity were one thing, but his renunciation of universal morality was inexcusable. But this is surely a farce that owes to a particular rendering of Christian theology that need not be defended in exact opposition to Nietzsche—and Copleston knew it. This incident from the pages of publishing history raises the question of Nietzsche's usefulness to Christian theology. Nietzsche would no doubt have laughed heartily at this anecdote since he clearly expected Christians to call him wicked. But even against Nietzsche's own wishes, can Christianity call him more than this? The aim of this volume is to enlarge on an affirmative answer to this question.

One hazard of writing on any topic appended with the words "and theology" is the implication that there is a singular discipline by that name. The existence of departments of theology and aisles (usually short) by that name in bookstores will no doubt help us to forgive those who assume that theology is rather a lot like anthropology or sociology. They too have departments and aisles in bookstores. But the subject of theology could not be more different—and more interesting—than these disciplines that take human existence as their starting point. Still, theologians are forever enticed by the advantages that attend to doing theology as though humanity is its subject. The manageability that attends to reducing theological discourse to human knowledge of God often cannot help but transmute into the study of human ways of knowing, meaning that theology ceases to be about God.

Even so, God is probably only rarely excluded from theology in an explicit manner and is instead more often made less and less divine through the transformation of the way theology is done. In writing on Nietzsche, I have wanted to avoid the implication that theology is a singular discipline precisely to the extent that "theology" names a temptation toward idolatry at best, and, at worst, is itself the greatest sin. Nietzsche disliked theologians for many of the same reasons that those who are described by that label ought also to dislike it.[2]

Insofar as theology purports to be a discourse about God, it will always be beset by the temptation to grasp at its object like the other discourses do. Its specialized language can make its object bend to fixed vocabulary and too-easily compartmental-ized sub-disciplines. For example, there is every indication that, for many years, biblical studies developed an autonomy from the-ology that entailed an increasingly complex set of quasi-scientific tools to aid its study quite apart from the lives of worship and devotion its object was meant to enable. But, of course, enabling is only one half of the function of biblical texts since part of what is involved in calling them scriptures is not only the acknowl-edgement that ways of life exist on the basis of these texts but, crucially, that these texts exist as scriptures on the basis of those ways of life. We may indeed be witnessing something of a reversal of this as Christian thought—owing no small debt to so-called "radical hermeneutics"—as it rediscovers an authentic voice with which to speak and study its scriptures as products of its practices of devotion.

Likewise, the lure for theology to exist as a self-sufficient discipline untouched by the vagaries of the concrete practices of those who engage in it can ultimately be too strong to resist. After all, in our desire for theology to be "like the other disciplines," those of us who teach and write theology can easily find ourselves dispensing with those aspects that rightly should make theology different, not least is the factor of God.[3]

In resisting this temptation, Nietzsche is an ally, though admittedly an unlikely one. Nietzsche loathed Christianity, especially Christian morality. He thought that Christians were irrational, self-deceived, repressed, and arrogant; he took Christian morality to be pettily reactionary and positively fatal to life; he had nothing but contempt for Paul and the apostles and fleetingly only slightly more to say in favor of Jesus. In his characteristically vitriolic prose, Nietzsche called Christianity "the one great curse, the one great innermost corruption . . . the one immortal blemish of mankind."[4] And yet Christians have learned nothing about God (their theologians, no doubt, having let them down) if they have not learned to look for God in unexpected places. Karl Barth famously rehearsed the untold ways that God can reveal himself: "through Russian communism, through a flute concerto, through a blossoming shrub or through a dead dog. We shall do well to listen to him if he really does so."[5] So also Christians find that, if they are to be a people who welcome unexpected gifts, they will likewise be hospitable to strangers like Nietzsche.

In addition, of course, it is his strangeness that holds the greatest promise. We need to be disarmed by this most singular houseguest. We are too in love with the sound of our own voices and too overcome with self-satisfaction at our cleverest formulations. Our words always threaten to harden into timeless assurances of our rightness, Cerberean guardians of our exalted reason. But Christians who read Nietzsche are offered willing assistance in chasing away these hounds.

The main reason that Nietzsche demands a Christian hearing does not finally reside in a lack of confidence in the Christian message, but corresponds to the fact that the truth of that very message demands such listening. This means that, as we listen, we will expect to hear *more* than is intended, particularly when our interlocutor is hostile to us. To be sure, Nietzsche could be hostile to Christians. Nevertheless, since God's truth is revealed in Jesus Christ, Christians may refuse to let such hostility have the final word. This is not because such hostility is misplaced (although it may be), but because hostility is an inappropriate stance to assume relative to God's good creation. Just as God's first word about creation was "good" because he created by and for his eternal Son, so also the final word is his eternal Son himself. In between, therefore, Christian thought is free to plunder every available resource in the confidence that the world belongs to Christ. And precisely because the one who owns the world is alive to it, a people who have learned to follow a risen Lord will expect to find him in unexpected places.

All of this is to say that the Christian ability to listen to Nietzsche as welcoming a stranger while also not letting what he "meant" have the final word will be a function of the strength of Christian devotion and the force of our conviction that the gospel is true. On this account, God has permitted that every text be read in light of the reality of Christ for better illuminating that reality. That we did not see it at first is only commentary on our blindness rather than the limited scope of the good news or of God's goodness.

It will already be apparent that this book is neither an objective survey nor an even-handed assessment. While I hope I have been fair, I have not pretended that fairness means dispassionately standing at a distance. There is too much at stake for that, not least of which is the honesty of our interests. In particular, I make use of Christian theological claims as premises in arguments and proceed from them in drawing conclusions. Nietzsche may have disagreed with both the claims and the conclusions, but he would have approved of the approach. *Stand within the strength of your convictions; if you fall down, at least it is not because you have tried to stand somewhere else.* The courage of standing with the truth is coterminous with the courage to subject the truth to the reality of your whole life, which is to say, your whole body. Nietzsche's fictional Zarathustra praises a fallen tightrope walker for this very courage. "You have made danger your vocation; there is nothing contemptible in that. Now you perish of your vocation: for that

I will bury you with my own hands."[6] In contrast, one who stands elsewhere has already admitted that one's so-called convictions are false. But at the same time, as Nietzsche would show, one's ability to stand for true convictions will always be an insufficient argument for their truth. If it were sufficient, we would have relied on a method of adjudication or some other criteria of assessing the truth of something that comes from outside the truth itself, thus making the truth less than true. What kind of philosophy makes such criteria more true (or more important) than the truth? Kant's, for one, does this; but it also pervades our thinking and characterizes our speech insofar as we persist in appealing to a surer foundation for what we ourselves claim and want others to believe.

Nietzsche knew that, while we may convince others, this fact only owes to their *taste*, that is, their proclivity for one option over another. But, of course, taste is not the same as mere choice, uninformed preference exercised willy-nilly in response to random stimuli, the testimony of others to the truth of their convictions being just one among many. Instead, the one whose spoken testimony is unavoidably bound up with the whole life of the speaker, which is to say, the self-involvement of his own person, may offer something convincing, though it can never be proof. "Proof" would only let the speaker off the hook with respect to his testimony by giving him something else to point to. He may duck out of the way and rely solely on the self-sustaining power of his claims. The irony, of course, is that any claims are *contingent* in both senses of the word: they depend on something that might not be there, in this case on the life of the speaker; and they are also non-necessary in the logical sense, which is to say, they do not purely follow from any premises.

In this way, we encounter the nature of Nietzsche's skepticism. It is not the radical self-questioning that, for Descartes, resulted from the drive for more indubitable forms of knowledge, less contingent declarations that owe to the necessary claims of reason. In contrast, Nietzsche is skeptical of this whole project, thinking that any necessary claims we discover will only be a function of our self-deception, our will to believe that we can rely on something less up for grabs than our own contingent existence and those factors by which we narrate our existence, for example, linguistically and historically. Our words and the stories we tell by means of them could have been otherwise—they are contingent. We convince ourselves that our words link up with objects in the world without remainder to control those objects and reassure ourselves that we are not at their mercy or else as subject as they are to chance encounters and haphazard possibilities. Our stories are grist for the mill of generalization and abstraction where we narcissistically feed fantasies about being characters in the most meaningful story in the universe, agents of the most important themes, and instruments of the most essential plots.

All the while, our language and our stories are made to function as necessary components in a larger logical or metaphysical structure that, as it turns out, only exists to corroborate the claims made within it, including, as it does, the means of assessing its own success. But if those means only represent a version of Kant's external assessment, they surely face the same skepticism that Nietzsche directed toward Cartesian knowledge. Descartes only satisfied himself that he had reached a level of knowledge free from contingency when he *convinced himself* that he had done so— on Nietzsche's critique, we would say that he had done so by lying to himself. Then it only takes transposing necessary claims of reason into another idiom or else hearing the stories others tell of the same event to topple the imposing tower that has encoded both knowledge and ways of knowing. In other words, when someone comes along who is not convinced that that level of knowledge is necessary, firm, and intuitive, there is nowhere for the argument to go. Modernity has labeled such voices as enemies or at least as irrational, often making them objects of violence. But if their existence is to be welcomed as modernity's philosophical other, Christian thought will find itself better suited to this task insofar as its hospitality is well practiced and to the extent that its own knowledge has nothing at stake in imposing towers.

The challenge, of course, is to pick up where this skepticism leaves off. This is no simple matter and it will occupy much of what follows in these pages. But here we may offer some preliminary observations about where theology "fits" in as part of a constructive thesis that assents to many of these critiques. First, theology cannot endure under any self-description that identifies it as a primary discourse. It is always and forever speech about the primacy of Christian practices, preeminently in worship and praise. On the eschatological horizon lies the end of theology—it, like God's people, being enfolded in prayer and praise for eternity. But God's people will not be extinguished like theology, the mere straw that will be burned, perhaps as holy incense at the throne of God, but burned nonetheless. There will then be nothing for theology to say since the people for whom it has been employed will confront theology's object face to face, that is, unmediated by words.[7] The immediacy of Christian worship to eternity with God reminds the practitioners of this humble discipline not only that the theological enterprise has a goal that includes its own obsolescence but also that the very practices that will make it obsolete are already a part of the church. Theology will therefore only be true to itself so long as it helps enable the church to worship *now* in truth.

This is what makes theology different from philosophy. The *philosopher*, whom Nietzsche called "the proudest of men," deserves this epithet because he imagines the work that he does to be of universal importance.[8] Philosophers are too arrogant, Nietzsche thinks, because philosophical knowledge constitutes and emerges from a realm of inquiry that cannot help but exalt only that kind of knowledge. To the extent, therefore, that having any kind of knowledge is connected with human arrogance at knowing anything, philosophers will be the most arrogant of them all since philosophy tells us what the most important kinds of knowledge are. Is it any wonder that Plato thought that philosophers should rule over us? It is not enough for them to be knowers, plain and simple, but philosophers must determine for everyone else which knowledge counts the most. Though it may sometimes seem as though theology is not much different from this, it will only be true to its object when it recognizes that there exists something between brute knowledge itself (which, of course, includes exalted knowledge) and the object of knowledge. For theology, what is in between are the people of God in worship.

Second, and related to this, it is necessary simply to admit that theology's task is therefore far from being a discipline in the normal sense. It must abjure the marks of the sort that so clearly characterize those disciplines that are manifestly academic, and that are academic precisely to the extent that they have these marks.

Theological knowledge fails to be appropriate to its object when it makes use of standard causal notions since these inevitably over-state what we can faithfully say about God. Every other discipline relates to an object that is part of the universe and, so long as theology aspires to be like these, it will reduce God to an aspect of creation. Put simply, when theology is a "discipline," it is so at the cost of making an idol out of God.

Both of these preliminary observations are correlative of the fact that the people of God are a people of a story. This is a story God tells and will bring to a conclusion. Only insofar as Christians are included in it by grace can we tell the story and claim that it is true. It is not true because we tell it; nor is it true because we know what it is for something to be true apart from the story we tell. Instead, the fact that we tell it is bound up with its truth. Theology, then, finds its proper home here: within the Christian proclamation since proclamation is the church's first mode of speech.[9] The church exists as a creation of the Holy Spirit, who breathed upon the disciples in the upper room, making them into apostles who spoke with tongues of fire. Christian speech is there-fore dependent on the action of God, making part of that speech's content the very confession that the church exists in front of the world with the very story for which it has been given such speech. In other words, the gospel is not just words *about* something in history but it is also partly a profession of faith that those who speak it are constituted by the very message they bear.

Therefore, if history has any meaning, it is in the form of *a people* in history rather than in the form of lessons to be learned from history. A people may indeed learn lessons, but only on the basis of first having been created as a people (and they will not learn them apart from this). We cannot pretend that Nietzsche would be happy with this, although he too located the meaning of history in a people—the *Übermensch* and those who produce him. Nevertheless he would no doubt also have suspected that to identify a people with the meaning of history can too easily underwrite our tendency for inflated self-importance inasmuch as we hastily declare, "We are that people!"

Yet a people are irreducibly concrete and do not yield to a metaphysically grandiose description. Being a member of a par-ticular people does not afford one a privileged place to stand but a socially embodied one that is imbued with stories and places. And as I said above, the claims of this people are concrete and historical (though in an admittedly complex, self-involving way) so that any metaphysical claims that emerge from them must pass through their embodied existence (though they will be no less metaphysical for this). It is likely that the particularity of this claim would have offended Nietzsche in his younger years more than later in his life. In the early essay "On Truth and Lies in the Nonmoral Sense" and also in *The Birth of Tragedy*, he disparages the mediating role that language plays, not only because it causes us to think that we have hold of surer knowledge than we really do but also because our language does not arise from the "essence of things." He holds up music in *BT* as the mode of discourse that most nearly approaches essences since it is non-linguistic and more intuitive than words. Nevertheless, he later abandoned the notion that there are essences, which he had presumably adopted from Kant and Schopenhauer, eventually claiming that essences do not exist at all since there are no uninterpreted facts: "facts are precisely what there is not, only interpretations."[10] This may have come to mean for Nietzsche that language is inevitable for our grasping of *all* things, not just concepts—but for particular things as well and it is therefore less heinous for it.[11]

To reiterate, Christian thought affirms the biblical narrative and its own situation within it which means that it affirms that God has not made contact with the world through necessary truths of reason but through a particular people. For example, it is not possible to know that God has made Israel into a people apart from the Hebrew witness, biblical and otherwise, just as it is not possible to know that God raised Jesus from the dead except through the words of witnesses, which is to say, through the speech of those for whom the resurrected Christ is a present reality. But this is also not to say that the church (much less Israel) is rendered *necessary* in any stronger sense of that word. There is nothing more epistemologically sure about the message it bears than its bearing of the message. It does not merely point to a metaphysical reality and then step out of the way since one comes to believe the message of the church by joining the church. The heresy of gnosticism was only a strategy for rendering the church redundant. At the same time, since the church was created by the Holy Spirit and is constantly upheld by the grace that continues to sustain all of creation, those who tell what can only be known through witness themselves only exist by gift. This means that the church can never be an argument. Its existence cannot be construed as part of a logical syllogism in which the conclusion is the truth that its mission is to proclaim to the world. This would only make the church's *existence* do the work of the church itself, which is irreducible.

This book treats some Christian topics that may be surprising to some readers, including the parables of Jesus and the Eucharist. There are already many books on Nietzsche and when they treat theological topics they can tend to cover a lot of the same ground. For example, it is common to approach the topic of religion by way of religious experience; the nature of God's being, and so on. These are important topics and others have treated them with great accomplishment.[12] However, while the present book does not avoid these ideas (the nature of God's being is discussed in Chapter 6), I have been most interested in areas that are perhaps more squarely within the Christian theological tradition or at least have closer ties to biblical themes. I admit that that distinction may not always bear the weight exerted against it, but I simply wanted to do something different on this occasion.

Therefore, I offer sample exhibits of what might materialize from walking with Nietzsche some distance. Some may feel that I have walked too closely to him, others that I have gone too far down his dangerous road, and still others may feel that I have tried too hard to make Nietzsche walk with me. Perhaps at times I have done all three. But I have wanted these exhibits to be ad hoc, even playful—a spirit I think Nietzsche encourages and enables.[13] And even when such playfulness may not be warranted by Nietzsche himself, surely theologians are relieved of taking their own discipline too seriously precisely because it is not their own.

I also want to be clear about what this book is not. It is not an introductory text to every aspect of Nietzsche's thought. Nietzsche wrote on an extraordinary number of topics and, while they usually make for rich reading themselves, the sheer variety does not always admit to patent connections or fruitful engagement at every level. It is perhaps most essential to indicate, likewise, that this book does not attempt a wholesale Christian critique of Nietzsche. For this reason, I have not primarily focused on the critiques he levels at Christianity, particularly as found in his later work *The Antichrist*. To be sure, his writings are alternately decorated and littered with critiques of Christianity, sometimes attended by gross misconceptions, unfair and ungenerous cavils on theological topics, time-bound reactions to the German Lutheran Christianity of the late nineteenth century and the women in his immediate family, and spiteful and acerbic taunts of major Christian figures (St. Paul is a "pernicious blockhead" and a "frightful swindler"[14]). These are really as serious as they are charming; they are also impossible to avoid and I do not attempt to ignore them by any means. Responding to Nietzsche's attacks on Christianity head-on is a worthy project and others have undertaken it with admirable thoroughness.[15] Even so, here I have given myself to what I hope is a constructive engagement that allows Nietzsche to assist Christianity to hone its own theological rhetoric, refine its felicity for proclaiming the evangel in harmonious rather than jarring tones, and fund an uncompromising and fearless self-criticism. This entails a caveat that, in these pages, there will necessarily be experiments and, I hope, munificent inquiries that will nevertheless fail to say everything that could, or even should, be said. Merold Westphal's suggestion that Christians do well to read Nietzsche during Lent as an aid to self-examination is a good one;[16] it names a style of reading and a trajectory of scrutiny I endorse even though only parts of this book were written during Lent, both as a matter of fact, and in its approach to our interlocutor.

Nietzsche can aid Christian reflection about Christianity's own confessions because of the content of those confessions. The whole world belongs to Christ whose reign is extensive enough, eminently capable of containing and narrating the rebellion of enemies. If God's way with the world were merely to vanquish his enemies, Christians might be permitted to ignore them, lock out the protesting and yet perishing voices, and be content with lovely in-house conversations. But surely these conversations would go nowhere. God's way with the world does not vanquish enemies but forgives them through non-violent love and suffering. It brings them inside, which cannot help but change the conversations.

However, there is also something about the spirit of Nietzsche himself that accords with the use that I attempt in this book.

I believe Michel Foucault was right to insist that those who write on Nietzsche do not serve the spirit of his life and work if they merely comment on and analyze what he has written. Thinking with Nietzsche, even thinking *against* Nietzsche, while not quickly dismissing how Nietzsche's spirit suffuses our criticism and protest, will indicate that we have learned something from him. Nietzsche does not need to be flattered by mere commentary; he would insist that what he said is not important, that he must be transcended and fascination with one man's words is a sign that we have taken ill, displaying the symptoms of a degenerate preoccupation with the past. As Foucault writes:

> I am tired of people studying [Nietzsche] only to produce the same kind of commentaries that are written on Hegel or Mallarmé. For myself, I prefer to utilize the writers I like. The only valid tribute to thought such as Nietzsche's is precisely to use it, to deform it, to make it groan and protest. And if the commentators then say that I am being faithful or unfaithful to Nietzsche, that is of absolutely no interest.[17]

Being faithful to Nietzsche may be of no interest, but faithfully grappling with him is. Accomplishing this in conjunction with faithfulness to Christian theology is not easy and I will not pretend to know that I have been successful at every turn; still, it is the task that I have undertaken.

Chapter 1

A catastrophic life[1]

Friedrich Nietzsche stopped receiving the Eucharist when he was 20 years old. He was a student, at home on a semester break from the University of Bonn. Whether his early life presaged good or ill for his relationship with Christianity is uncertain. When he was not yet five years old, his father, a Lutheran pastor, died of "softening of the brain." A year later, the family moved from the small German village of Röcken to Naumberg where, at school, the other pupils called Nietzsche "the little pastor" owing to the skill and passion with which he recited hymns and verses from the Bible. Christianity ran deep in his family who expected him to become a pastor like his father; for a short time he even studied theology before settling on the study of philology.

Nietzsche's decision to stop taking Communion was made to the utter chagrin of his mother and it no doubt coincided with his rather determined urgings to his sister to question the Christian tradition in which they had both been reared. Writing to her in 1865, he cast their childhood faith in God in his newly deployable terms of the heroic truth-teller and truth-seeker who takes nothing for granted, particularly if continuing in belief allows one to repose in the comfort of the unexamined life.

> [I]s it really so difficult simply to accept everything in which one has been brought up, which has gradually become deeply rooted in oneself, which holds true among relatives and among many good people, which does moreover really comfort and elevate man? Is that more difficult than to take new paths, struggling against habituation, uncertain of one's independent course, amid frequent vacillations of the heart, and even of the conscience, often comfortless, but always pursuing the eternal goal of the true, the beautiful, the good?

Is it then a matter of acquiring the view of God, world, and atonement in which one can feel most comfortable? Is it not, rather, true that for the true researcher the result of his research is of no account at all? Do we, in our investigations, search for tranquility, peace, happiness? No—only for the truth, even if it were to be frightening and ugly.[2]

Though he found it disturbingly problematic in some respects, Nietzsche was always captivated by what he was later to refer to as the will to truth, the determination and courage to embrace the truth no matter how unpleasant. He was praised for his genius as a student and moved from Bonn to Leipzig, following his great mentor Ritschl there. At Leipzig, Nietzsche discovered the philosophy of Schopenhauer who dramatically influenced his will to create: "The categorical imperative 'Thou shalt and must write' has roused me."[3] The following year, he met Richard Wagner who shared an interest in Schopenhauer and Nietzsche ecstatically embraced a friendship with the famous composer. The twin influences of Schopenhauer and Wagner on Nietzsche cannot be exaggerated; Nietzsche's first book, *The Birth of Tragedy from the Spirit of Music*, was a homage to Wagner's music, extolling it for rekindling in modern life the greatness of Greece. As a critical work of philology, however, the book was a disaster. Even Ritschl ridiculed it. In time, however, Nietzsche would come to distance himself from both Schopenhauer and Wagner.

Nietzsche had shortly before been appointed to the University of Basel where he quickly became disappointed by the quality of his students and the lackluster reception his writing was receiving. Starting in 1873, he began to suffer from bouts of illness—possibly related to a short tour of duty he served in the Franco-Prussian War as a medic—that would plague him for the rest of his life, making his mood melancholy and his outlook grim: "My father died of an inflammation of the brain at age thirty-six. It is possible that it will happen to me even faster."[4] In 1876, he was granted a leave of absence from Basel for his illness and for several years worked on *Human, All Too Human* while intermittently returning to Basel to teach. When the book was published in 1878, Wagner disapproved strongly and Nietzsche also expressed his disapproval at Wagner's new opera *Parsifal*, accusing it of being too Christian.

For the next ten years, Nietzsche lived the itinerant life of a wanderer, moving to warmer Mediterranean climes in the winter and often spending summers hiking the Swiss Alps. He resigned from Basel, his illness thoroughly making any teaching impossible; he was granted an annual pension. The thoughts now seemed to come more quickly and fluidly: Nietzsche's greatest insights would often come during extended mountain walks when he would pause to scribble on a notepad. His remark that "only thoughts reached by walking have value" indicates the importance of experience for knowledge that gave shape to his fervent belief that knowledge is always secondary to life itself.[5] He knew that this was antithetical to the philosophical spirit of the age. The modern proclivity for modes of discourse that attempt to eradicate the contingencies of the individual encounter *in time* produced a "universal" philosophical style—the great Enlightenment dream. But Nietzsche saw this style as a mere ruse for the abandonment of life, a refusal to think while walking, as it were. Metaphysics always threatens to overpower the simplicity of objects and ideas that otherwise develop in the soil of lived lives.

However, life was also increasingly difficult with Nietzsche's illness and so he chose to live like an ascetic often for the sake of ideas. As a university student, he had subjected himself to mild disciplines: he stopped eating meat and gave up tobacco and alcohol. Self-mastery was to remain with him in many forms, crucially sustaining his frenzied writing in later years and even adorning some of his most profound ideas about life. In a letter to his friend, Franz Overbeck (1882), he admits to a drive to overcome the tension between opposing passions:

> I am exerting every ounce of my self-mastery; but I have lived in solitude too long and fed too long off my "own fat," so that I am now being broken, as no other man could be, on the wheel of my own passions. If only I could sleep![6]

Nietzsche's will to see things as they really are, apart from the clouds of metaphysics, grew stronger. He was aware that this will demands great courage and a life lived in unwavering determination to confront everything that is objectionable. "People who comprehend a thing to its very depths," he wrote, "rarely stay faithful to it for ever. For they have brought its depths into the light of day: and in the depths there is always much that is unpleasant to see."[7] Philosophers, he deduced, are cowardly for their tendency to catch up particulars into greater totalizing wholes. Still, the reason that Nietzsche derided philosophy in this regard was that he actually found it too theological. The theologian, he said, is his antithesis and "I have dug up the theologians' instinct everywhere."[8] As rich as was the inheritance of Western thought and culture, it was imbued with theological concepts, convictions, and presuppositions.

Nietzsche's famous quip that "I fear we still believe in God because we believe in grammar" is expanded by Derrida in the claim that "the age of the sign is essentially theological."[9] What has led us to assume that existences always may designate a more fundamental order that we can grasp and array conceptually? How can we account for our acute trust in the serviceability of concepts if not by way of underlying, culturally stabilizing theology?

Nietzsche needed to do little more than name it. He may thus be considered a cultural despiser, one whose orientation to human existence was intentionally set at odds to the orientation of the products humans had hitherto produced for themselves as enduring features passed on from generation to generation. His response to culture was more fundamental than a simple rejection of God; it called for the reorganization of the philosophical principles that lay unexamined behind a culture that had, at best, an ambiguous relationship with the past and, at worst, was confused and cowardly. Nietzsche could not bear any philosophy that did not serve life. He despised those for whom philosophical thinking replaced actual living insofar as such thinking is either ancillary to life or else actually functions as a way of evading life's opportunities and demands. The irony of a culture simultaneously enamored with progress and quick to sanction a particular and convenient reading of the past was not lost on Nietzsche.

His final productive years were filled by a frenetic torrent of ideas, sparkling with brilliance as much as disclosing loose associations and sometimes careless or petty grudges. He was embarrassed by his youthfully excessive enchantment with both Schopenhauer and Wagner and took steps to refute both on a variety of grounds including re-narrating the significance of the writings he had produced while under their influence. By the time that the intellectual world started to take real notice in Nietzsche's philosophy and it was even beginning to be granted a degree of respectability, he was in no mental state to appreciate it. He spent his last decade utterly dependent on the care of his mother and sister and, apart from brief periods of lucidity, reduced to incurable madness.

Chapter 2
Un-mastering knowledge

Nietzsche's account of knowledge is intimately linked with themes that run through all of his writings but that are perhaps most evident in early texts. What is the relationship between truth and knowledge? What, if anything, enables our knowing to be adequate to the thing known? These cardinal questions of modern epistemology, Nietzsche thought, not only yield inadequate answers, but the modern mind already erred in presuming that they are the right questions to ask and that, by answering them correctly, the mind's aspirations might be sustained and authorized. We may immediately inflect the force of these questions' inadequacy toward theological concerns by interrogating the nature of theological knowledge along Barthian lines where there are several precise intersections with Nietzsche.

Consider the following theological claim: *Christianity has no particular stake in the idea of truth, truth-as-such, or in defending theories of truth.* As a claim, it cannot be obviously true even while the reason for it is simple enough: it can be stated (and has been stated) apart from making any connections whatsoever with the actual content of the Christian confession. It is therefore a thoroughly Barthian objection that Christians do not believe in "the truth" but in the God of Abraham and Jesus. Moreover, Christians do not believe that Jesus is the truth because of a prior understanding of what it means for something to be true. Instead, Christian thinking about knowledge and truth begins with confessions made irrespective of theory. To be sure, Christians have not been immune from the fascination of showing how something can be known and how it can be known to be true. Saint Augustine worked with an argument that sought to prove the existence of truth: if truth perished, it would be true that truth had perished, meaning that truth cannot perish.[1] Likewise, Duns Scotus argued that the existence of truth is known directly and not inferred (though he still argues the point): if truth did not exist, it would still be true that truth did not exist; therefore, truth exists.[2]

The risk involved in making arguments of this kind is that they can suggest that either a theory of truth or an argument for the existence of truth is more important than truth, which is to say, that such arguments and theories are more valuable precisely because they are more rational than any single truth they are meant to describe. Among Barth's many statements of this view, his Christological formulations of it are most poignant.

> It goes without saying that if the truth is sundered from the true Witness [Jesus Christ], if it is made the mere idea of intercourse between God and man, then, however perfectly it may be thought out and presented, it is not the truth. And if its Witness is only its Witness, its manifestation and symbol, then, however highly He may be exalted as such, He is not the true Witness.[3]

Whatever precariousness has befallen Christian thought through the ages when it found itself venturing *a priori* theorems of knowledge's truth like Augustine's and Scotus's, the risk has certainly been radically transformed into thoroughgoing enchantment where modern accounts of epistemology gained prominence. In the modern idiom, anything true comes to be subordinated to accounts of truth and therefore subject to them. We are prevented (or prevent ourselves) from knowing something unless it can be proven to be "knowable." This fascination is the object of one of Nietzsche's earliest critiques and, though it is transformed throughout his writings, it is nevertheless a concern that animates his work throughout.[4]

Modern theorizing about knowledge can be traced back to Descartes who had what might be called a two-stage epistemology. There is what you know and also how you know it, knowledge itself and the theory of knowledge employed to justify that knowledge. In his first published work, *The Birth of Tragedy*, Nietzsche does not specifically target this epistemology as problematic, but instead likens Descartes to the Greek tragedian, Euripides, and then indicts both thinkers for sharing a flawed approach to truth and knowledge that jeopardizes what one actually wants to say is true or known. Both make theoretical appeals such as Euripides' appeal to divine trustworthiness to justify the fact that what is disclosed to us as real is true. How do we know that what the gods say about the world is true? The answer is because the gods tell the truth. Like any exchange that concerns a justification of knowledge, this is a two-stage question and answer; in this case, the truth of divine disclosure is ultimately made to answer to the *truth of the truthfulness* of the gods. In dramatic theater, Euripides introduces the Prologue as a new development within the tradition of Greek tragedy. Here, an omniscient narrator plainly sets the scene and delineates the major turns of the plot which are to come, describes the principal characters, and enumerates the story's antecedents. Nietzsche takes this to be an aberrant departure from the subtlety used by the earlier tragedians (notably Aeschylus and Sophocles) to convey necessary information to the audience in the opening scenes of the play.[5]

For Nietzsche, Euripides therefore represents (indeed himself pioneered) a rationalistic turn. Most obviously, in the tragedian, a condescension is made to the audience, mitigating their feeling of suspense, of what may happen next. Euripides focused on powerfully rendering the plot with lyrical force independent of the audience's sense of anticipation for certain outcomes of the plot. His appeal to the mind of the audience, however forceful in its display, merely nurtured the understanding. But "understanding kills action," ultimately letting the audience off the hook as potential participants in the tragic themes enacted before their eyes.[6] It is ironic then, at least from Nietzsche's point of view, that Euripides is sometimes celebrated for his seemingly closer connection with the audience (putting the audience itself on stage, as it were, because of more obviously pandering to its needs for explanation). In fact, the tragedian is actually cheating the audience out of its own involvement in the narrative insofar as suspense and not knowing might otherwise themselves be constitutive plot elements. Nevertheless, by its very nature, these things were only ever elements irreducible to conveying information such as the Prologue later sought to provide. Nietzsche surely critiques Euripides for this, even impugning him for the "end of tragedy!"[7]

We may notice how the *purpose* of the narrative itself changes once it has been demythologized. No longer can the story serve to draw its hearers into its course of events, linked by suspense, by contingent relations that are experienced by the audience as matters of existential urgency, and not only for the audience but also for everyone whose fate is bound up with the narrative's outcome. The net effect of Euripides' rationalism, in other words, is the elimination of any genuinely tragic elements while what Nietzsche extols in earlier tragedy are simply those characteristics that allow tragedy to resemble life itself, in all of its unknowns and disorder. Euripides might have agreed with the fact that a demythologized narrative in fact functions this way but that this is immaterial to its purpose which was only ever lyrical and epic to begin with, which is to say that what matters, after all, are the events of the plot, the consciousness of the *individual* audience member, and the lyrical vigor of the presentation.[8] These can be achieved most efficiently by detemporalizing the very scope of the narrative events. So long as the wonder, suspense, and intrigue of the audience are irrelevant to the course of the narrative, the plot may actually be "spoiled" at an early stage (namely, in the Prologue itself) without loss. But, for Nietzsche, the loss is great indeed: the power of myth is lost, the audience is robbed of genuine involvement and instead witnesses a complete sham.

> What were you thinking of, overweening Euripides, when you hoped to press myth, then in its last agony, into your service? It died under your violent hands; but you could easily put in its place an imitation that, like Heracles's monkey, would trick itself out in the master's robes. . . . [T]hough you pointed and burnished a sophistic dialectic for the speeches of your heroes, they have only counterfeit passions and speak counterfeit speeches.[9]

In the twentieth century, narrative theology rightly developed a way of disdaining both a merely detemporalized and also a facilely rationalistic (and therefore didactic and propositionalist) approach to Christian belief. The net effect of the rationalism it abjured has always been that Christian belief is inevitably reduced to "believing stuff," a Gnostic perversion and constant temptation for Christian thought in which there can ultimately be no new life, Christianity having been condensed into a mere philosophy. Having become a knowledge, life itself is degraded to a known quantity in which the solutions to world problems take the form of further knowledge. Nietzsche saw how this leads to the assumption that life should be guided by science and what we might call a confidence in technology with which we turn to life smilingly and say, "I want you. You are worth knowing."[10] How would we know that life is worth knowing ahead of time if not for the prior conviction that what we will encounter will be easily accommodated within a fairly limited purview and from among a paltry set of possibilities? It is the *possibilities* which, for Nietzsche, constitute our greatest illusion. And, of course, we must uphold the illusion that life is a known quantity if we are committed to a form of knowledge that masters its objects.

For example, Nietzsche contrasts a commendable Dionysian spirit that renders life appropriately full of contingency with the later spirit of Apollo that became expressed in Alexandrian Greece. The latter "Socratic culture" was marked by a misplaced optimism in knowledge that turns out actually to be a belief in omniscience. The belief that a complete book of knowledge could be written rests on prior assumptions about the simplicity of the world and the predictability of ordinary causality. Nietzsche notes that there is a kind of theology at work here that achieves "metaphysical solace" and contends that, despite the apparent disorder of the world, there is nevertheless an underlying unity, rationality, and order available even for anthologizing.[11] Sculpture is an example of an art form that has all the marks of the Apollonian spirit: the clean lines convey the rationality of nature's form, its clear ordering according to established patterns and clear laws; the perfect splendor of its celebrated subjects express the confidence that, beneath it all, things in the world are more beautiful than they appear and sculpture brings to the surface the true nature of things normally only reserved for hidden depths; the simplicity of the subject—the sole figure on grand display—discloses the strength of the individual as the exclusive locus of human greatness, both the smallest and largest unit of ideal life.

The spirit of sculpture is the consoling spirit of Apollo that trades in fables about true reality which is Dionysian and visible *at the surface*, never beneath it: "the 'true world' has been constructed out of contradiction to the actual world: indeed an apparent world, insofar as it is merely a moral-optical illusion."[12] Moreover, there is a cost involved in all of this image-making: the effort needed to sustain the illusion and set before each other and ourselves a world unseen and yet somehow more real. The illusion's social expression, Nietzsche observes, is difficult to manage:

> One thing should be remembered: Alexandrian culture requires a slave class for its continued existence, but in its optimism it denies the necessity for such a class; therefore it courts disaster once the effect of its nice slogans concerning the dignity of man and the dignity of labor have worn thin.[13]

Slogans of human dignity are marshaled against the reality of social injustice and, worse than that, even the *necessity* of social injustice. Therefore, Nietzsche not only holds that the slogans are untrue but also that they serve an ideological function, allowing such a society to live with itself despite the appearance of contradiction—and precisely insofar as that society is able to point to the contradiction as *just* an appearance. The narratival enactment that tragedy achieves not only posits nothing more fundamental than the narrative it enacts, but in doing so, it also averts the specters of ideology.

When Christian thought drew attention to narrative, it grasped a parallel insight to Nietzsche's. It refused to overlook the details of real history and other stories as mere appearances that allowed us to downgrade the significance of detail on the pretext that we were really only interested in the metaphysical substrate. But it is necessary to explore some aporias that appear for Christian thought. One that will be discussed in Chapter 6 turns on the question of the real nature of reality's contingency, whether Christian thought might affirm the random chaos of absolute flux, and the possibility of an alternative Trinitarian account that Nietzsche surely could not fathom or countenance. Here we may simply ask whether there is a necessary connection between contingency and tragedy.[14] It must be remembered that in Greek theater, tragedy does not simply mean "sad" or "regrettable." Instead, it is an artistic rendering of and confrontation with the forces of the world that are beyond our knowledge and control and where an attendant epistemology, for Nietzsche at least, is properly sundered from grasping. In his words, "The tragic artist is no pessimist: he is precisely the one who says Yes to everything questionable, even to the terrible—he is *Dionysian*."[15] Prior to Homer, it did not occur to the Greeks to ask about the point of suffering (as Achilles does in the *Iliad*); the only question was how to live with it. Nietzsche takes this noble spirit to have been corrupted once the question of the *meaning* of suffering is allowed somehow to take on greater urgency than the *endurance* of suffering. With this shift, it is not so much that now meanings were sought that assist endurance, but that the whole question of there being a meaning in the first place is bound up with a diminished nobility, that is, defeated efforts to endure.

Even though he was no mere votary of Dionysus, Aeschylus earned Nietzsche's obvious admiration for producing tragedies that refuse to tame the wildness of the infamous god. In particular, Nietzsche's admiration extends through to the subject matter of one of these tragedies, the myth of Prometheus. It is a myth that concerns the fundamental and interminable conflict between humanity and the gods and the question of how humans too may lay hold of the power of fire—that obdurate force conventionally only at divine disposal. In the face of the gods, Promethian virtue extols "an exalted notion of active sin" and tragedy names the suffering that comes from this sin. "The tragedy at the heart of things . . . the contrariety at the center of the universe" is a function of the interface between the divine and the human in which both are asserting themselves, both are in the right, and therefore both must suffer.[16] Such suffering is neither quite commendable nor quite regrettable. Instead, it is the expected outcome of "that primordial contradiction" against which one learns "both to sin and to suffer." In spirit, the Prometheus myth is profoundly Dionysian. Moreover, the conflict of Prometheus would remain *purely* Dionysian except for Aeschylus's Apollonian attempt to appeal to justice for rendering it intelligible. This prompts Nietzsche to summarize the

Aeschylean Prometheus using this formula: "Whatever exists is both just and unjust, and equally justified in both." He then glosses the formula: "What a world!"[17] Against its best and original ends, this tragedy therefore grants its own kind of metaphysical comfort to those who insist on living life in the face of the tragic reality that life is a suffering that cannot be escaped.

Despite the mixed record of tragedy as a genre, the tragic reality of life may, on its own, nevertheless still sound a lot like a metaphysical doctrine but for the fact that Nietzsche consistently denied having such doctrines, a denial found especially in his later writings. He believed that once metaphysics is purged, all that remains is a chaotic surge of random forces. Like the impermanence of fire with its ever-changing flames and lack of continuous substance, Nietzsche's world is in constant flux. And for him, this is not only true at the level of observation; it is not only what the world looks like to us while maintaining a deeper constancy. It is all that there is. We see flux because flux is the nature of things; and when we do not see it, this is only because we have believed illusions. In all of this, though, can it have escaped Nietzsche that such a view is itself metaphysical? Surely it is a belief about the way things are and what there is (*the* metaphysical questions) to hold that flux is the nature of things. Nietzsche wanted to say that things have no nature and their not-having-a-nature is evidence of a fundamental chaos. In this regard, exposing the illusion that culture is the only reality is one function of tragedy but ironically, the *enjoyment* of tragedy or listening to music (which for Nietzsche, ideally should amount to the same thing) is a participation in the chaos of existence, enjoyment that clearly must take some form of "Isn't this wonderful!" And what is wonderful? It is the celebration of life's contingency and ultimate purposelessness. But, whatever else it may be, might it not also be an experience of a kind of metaphysical comfort?

Thus, two elements of *The Birth of Tragedy* seemingly undermine Nietzsche's attempt to do without metaphysics: one is the metaphysics of flux and contingency and the other is the comfort (or at least joy) that derives from coming to terms with flux and contingency through celebrating them as the way things are.[18] The second of these two, of course, might simply be seen as proving Nietzsche's point about the consolation metaphysics brings.

On the other hand, it may be objected that while a metaphysics of essences brings comfort, other things do as well. Accordingly, just because we take solace in the unmediated, artistic experience of the world as it is, we also find repose in lies and illusions—this does not mean that all illusions function for us at the level of metaphysics, though many do. In later works, Nietzsche's position retains the tragic element while attempting to deliver an account that can resist the charge of metaphysics more thoroughly.[19]

What makes some kind of metaphysics inescapable in a discussion of knowledge, even for Nietzsche, is the drive to conceptualize that which is inherently beyond comprehension. Nietzsche wants to maintain that reality cannot be grasped through knowledge as knowledge is always more limited than that which it attempts to describe. In his view, this was Socrates' mistake, perhaps as when in *Phaedrus*, the pied piper of Athens asks:

> But of the heaven which is above the heavens, what earthly poet ever did or ever will sing worthily? It is such as I will describe; for I must dare to speak the truth, when truth is my theme.[20]

Yet Nietzsche thinks Socrates attempts the impossible, only appearing to succeed. After all, reality is *greater* than knowledge and can only be "known" through experience, truly living life, welcoming its fullest expressions, and refusing to preclude any experience in advance of it. In one aphorism, Nietzsche reproves the tree of knowledge for failing to be the tree of life.[21] The tree of knowledge trades in "probability but no truth" precisely because its fruit is insufficient to sustain life. This sundering of knowledge from life is not primarily a disparagement of knowledge but an exaltation of life's abundance that can never be captured on a tree (where one knows to return, for example, when a certain kind of fruit is desired and all that remains is to pluck it; this knowledge is *probability*). To know something ahead of time is already, in a sense, to have experienced it, if only through anticipation. But truly to be open to the unknown involves an epistemological humility about the possibilities, not only for the future but also about what there *is* in the first place. For Nietzsche, this necessarily leads to an appropriately uncertain metaphysics. If metaphysics asks

"What is there?" then the very form of the question invites an answer squarely from within the domain of epistemology since any answer is nothing other than an indication of where "what there is" is grasped by the mind. Even to answer the question with "We do not *know*" makes this plain. Therefore, Nietzsche cannot be (at least in *The Birth of Tragedy*) against metaphysics as such—we may in fact read him as appealing for the ascendancy of metaphysics over against knowledge: the former is unbounded, abundant, inexhaustible, free; the latter is limited, constrained, confined, truncated.

Nevertheless, the matter is not as simple as this. It is one thing to attest to the abundance of reality over against knowledge. But is such a move not in some sense closer to a grasping knowledge than to sheer experience? Put differently, if reality is not subject to the purview afforded it by the canons of knowledge, how would Nietzsche or anyone else know it?

This question needs to be addressed in two respects. First, it shows how Kantian Nietzsche is since it plays into a Kantian distinction that Nietzsche upholds, at least for some time: the distinction between essence and appearance (of things-in-themselves and things).[22] Our knowledge is limited to grasping appearances; but if what lies beneath them is always in constant flux, it is futile to think that essences (absolute reality) might be captured by codes and canons of knowledge. It is simply not possible to know something that is in flux. Again, the Promethian myth furnishes the image of fire that Nietzsche would have appreciated for its Buddhist resonances of impermanence. In this image, as before, reality is as a fire, constantly shifting flames, a blaze of endlessly altering traces—the fire is nothing other than the flames, meaning that strictly speaking, there is no "fire" at all. And since they are constantly shifting, one can only *know* flames by grasping at their fading existences as instantiated in the past and accounted for only using statistics. But this kind of knowledge (history and statistics) does not finally get at the reality of fire; it only tells us about what *these particular* flames have done and been like. Attempts to project into the future arise out of a confidence that if things have happened a particular way before they will therefore do so again. Such knowledge is metaphysical exactly because of this confidence.

We may grant the impossibility of relying on standard causality of this sort to give us future knowledge (which is also to say *present* knowledge since any confidence that arises from accounts of how things usually happen, strictly speaking and even at its best, only applies to the *past*). Yet this raises the second respect in which we must address the question we posed above, namely, concerning who could know that reality is greater than knowledge: it is a misleading question because it already presupposes the ascendancy of knowledge. Embedded in its logic is the assumption that a *knowledge* must certify knowledge, that any account of validating the possibility of knowing one thing must be delivered up in a form that is itself antecedently verified in exactly the same respect. The objection is only sustained as legitimate when it conforms to the conviction that the ability to know something (or better, *knowing* the ability to know something) warrants and justifies knowing that thing. This is a version of the two-tier epistemology with which Descartes ushered in modern philosophy.

Therefore, it is clear that Nietzsche's critique of Socratic knowledge is really a critique of modern philosophy's fascination with epistemological questions. The two-tier epistemology of modernity was essentially a *skeptical* position because it sought to subject all knowledge to fewer and fewer rational claims. For Descartes, there was finally only one such claim: the foundational function of reason itself. This is sometimes thought to have been a desperate move that he made inadvisably, since in fact, there is no such foundation at all. Descartes simply could not bear that conclusion.[23] Still, the prevailing dogma of the nineteenth-century university system Nietzsche knew located authority in the *form* knowledge took among those who functioned as its experts, namely, those enshrined in prestigious university posts. When he wrote *The Birth of Tragedy*, Nietzsche was yet to abandon his post in classical philology at Basel, but with the book, he had in some ways already spurned it. Among his colleagues at Germany's important universities, reviews of the book ranged from dismissive to damning. Its complete lack of a traditional, scholarly apparatus and wildly unsubstantiated claims enraged not a few academics. However, even though Nietzsche would later come to share some of these same critiques, particularly those he attributed to his youthful excess, the style of the book was actually crucial to its argument. As a judgment upon modernity, the book could not simultaneously rely on the well-established procedures according to which modern knowledge erected itself as authoritative and therefore *true*. In his time, Nietzsche was quite alone in reading the Greeks to be anything other than an ancient congratulatory gloss on modern European culture.

If the skeptical modern motto was "Question everything," then Nietzsche's appeal was for a different motto: "Nothing is what it seems." We are the worst judges of our own actions because our motives are too bound up with them and we are perennially blind to them.[24] It is a mistake to think that we could separate our will from our actions since there are no actions apart from will and, though Nietzsche famously theorized about pure will (a train of thought adapted from Schopenhauer), willing is likewise only ever instantiated in actions. Therefore,

> the decisive value of an action resides in precisely that which is *not intentional* in it, and that all that in it which is intentional, all of it that can be seen, known, "conscious", still belongs to its surface and skin—which, like every skin, betrays something but *conceals* still more[.] In brief, we believe that the intention is only a sign and symptom that needs interpreting.[25]

This work of interpretation is not just the straightforward skepticism of the modern mind that questions everything. But it corresponds to a new kind of analysis that Nietzsche called genealogy.[26] Genealogy tells a story of origins that does not appeal to transcendent truths, whether the *a priori* givens that function syllogistically (such as so-called analytic statements that are true by definition: "all unmarried men are bachelors") or religious claims known by divine revelation. As a purely immanentist way of proceeding, genealogy makes an argument by showing how the claims of the present have a this-worldly past (though such a past may be mythic as it always is for Nietzsche, though much less so for someone like Michel Foucault who operates with real history, despite Foucault's claim to be writing fictions).

In former times, one sought to prove that there is no God—today one indicates how the belief that there is a God could *arise* and how this belief acquired its weight and importance: a counter-proof that there is no God thereby becomes superfluous.[27]

The counter-proofs are hiding something that they cannot see, namely, the motives of those who proffer them. But genealogy exposes them, making it "the definitive refutation." As he concludes,

When in former times one had refuted the "proofs of the existence of God" put forward, there always remained the doubt whether better proofs might not be adduced than those just refuted: in those days atheists did not know how to make a clean sweep.[28]

Nietzsche's definitive refutation is of use to Christian thought for chastening an overzealous knowledge that assumes that God can be proven and demonstrated by logic. It is obvious that he had a distaste for the God of Christianity as he understood him, but this led Nietzsche to an insight about God's provability and believ-ability that should be heeded: "If one were to *prove* this God of the Christians to us, we should be even less able to believe in him."[29] A proven God must be less than God, since he would be captive to human reason and fitted to the bounds of our knowledge—therefore an idol of precisely the sort that endured Nietzsche's philosophical hammer. Just as Nietzsche's famous madman does not herald the non-existence of God, but his death, Christianity does not depend on God's mere *existence*, but crucially on his *life*.[30] And proving the existence of a living God cannot finally be accomplished in the form of an intellectual exercise without fal-sifying its own claims, making God who is living and free into a dead, staid object to be enslaved by knowing minds. It is on these grounds that Barth heralded the end of religion: "But religion must die. In God we are rid of it."[31] Hans Urs von Balthasar adduced that this placed Barth "dangerously close to Nietzsche."[32]

If Nietzsche's definitive refutation takes a genealogical form, then asking how someone can know that reality is greater than knowledge cannot really be an objection to Nietzsche without actually proving his point about the status of knowledge in modernity. The very form of the question privileges the outcome in favor of epistemological supremacy: *if something cannot be demonstrated as knowable, then it cannot be known at all.* This is a thoroughly modern theorem owing to Descartes; and yet we may recall how it also betrays Euripides' similar dependence on the truth of divine disclosure for knowing the truth about reality.

Even so, Nietzsche holds out for an alternative to this kind of knowledge, a deeper, more intuitive and emotional connection to the reality of things that is beyond all rational justification and yet is not to be despised for it. This "Dionysian wisdom" is a knowledge without grasping, without mastery. Such Dionysian wisdom is, for Nietzsche, the power necessary to endure Dionysian reality.[33] As we have seen, it is of little use to ask how we know that reality is Dionysian since to do so discloses our reliance on a form of knowledge inferior to Dionysian wisdom. There is unquestionably something circular about Nietzsche's argument in this regard and one wonders whether he is just not playing fair. At the least, however, we may say that reality-as-Dionysian is simply a given for Nietzsche, even though it may not be rationally defensible, which in fact partially seems to be the point.[34] He refuses to proceed according to a Socratic dialectic.

The aphoristic style that Nietzsche adopted in his middle works (notably *HH* and *D*, though continuing on in some fashion through *BGE*) is a deliberate stylistic departure from argument and, as such, intentionally means to embody Dionysian wisdom. An aphorism does not step through logic or otherwise lead the reader along a chain of reasoning; it is simply there to be disposed of in any way. It is probably no coincidence that the works in this period are considered more pronouncedly psychological than Nietzsche's others. He intended to confront the reader with an aphoristic *event*, with words that could immediately be taken either to be plausible or implausible. Those unconvinced, Nietzsche surely reasoned, would no more be convinced by a drawn-out, conventional essay. Why bother with a philosophical and academic charade when the root is psychological? Therefore, Nietzsche believed he was undercutting dialectic's intrinsic affinity for our self-fascination, in which we are able to convince ourselves that we are actually doing some productive work by thinking. After a long series of arguments, if one claims to be convinced, might it simply have been an extended exercise in narcissism: prejudice plus words and time? With aphorism, Nietzsche was attempting drastically to reduce words and time to expose prejudice, our most profoundly *philosophical* faculty.[35]

For this reason, it appears contradictory when Nietzsche acknowledges that in order for aphorism to work properly, it must, in a sense, be allowed to function free of psychologizing. This is not the place, he avers, for readers to engage in *ad hominems*.

> *Readers of aphorisms.* The worst readers of aphorisms are the author's friends if they are intent on guessing back from the general to the particular instance to which the aphorism owes its origin; for with such pot-peeking they reduce the author's whole effort to nothing; so that they deservedly gain, not a philosophic outlook or instruction, but—at best, or at worst—nothing more than the satisfaction of vulgar curiosity.[36]

Nietzsche does not want his friends to act as archaeologists, deconstructing his aphorisms. However, this concern does not arise amidst any hopes harbored for taking refuge in modern-esque generalities through the uttering of timeless principles; he famously opposes attempts of this kind. For example, he chides philosophers for a lack of historical sense, mistaking mere millennia of human existence for what is eternally human. As a species, we have been around much longer than this and it is surely a function of our arrogance that we take as normative those aspects of being human that are only humanity's recent history. Against this, "there are *no eternal facts*, just as there are no absolute truths. Consequently what is needed from now on is *historical philosophizing*, and with it the virtue of modesty."[37]

He is therefore not concerned with countenancing otherwise inexorable meanings of aphorisms. Instead, his concern is with the aborted *experience* of the reader, who cheats herself out of an authentic encounter—of her own particular interface with the aphoristic truth. Far from being a universal that mediates a multitude of such particular encounters, the aphorism is nothing other than the meanings it takes precisely in these encounters. Just as a prophet is without honor in his hometown, Nietzsche worried that his friends would short-circuit this process and literally rob what he was writing of its meaning insofar as they sought to find meaning in the author's existence rather than their own.[38] This is mere "vulgar curiosity." In this respect, Nietzsche is not really rejecting the *ad hominem* after all; he is, in fact, appealing to it. Anything less is pathetic pot-looking.[39]

It seems clear that Nietzsche did not want to function as writer and author of aphorisms; he wanted to be an aphorism himself. He positively enjoyed the prospect of being loved or hated *as himself*. He therefore sought to insert himself so thoroughly throughout his writing that it would become impossible to accept what he was saying without also accepting him. As with an aphorism, one must take him or leave him. Zarathustra did not want it to be possible for his followers to find him but not having found themselves.[40] Nietzsche knew that this strategy could not but appear decidedly unphilosophical—and he was enthralled by it. He did not want to convince so much as wound or delight (or both).[41]

Very little in the Christian tradition has aphoristic form. The particular ways that God has been present with a particular people (the Jews) and with consummate intensity in Palestine in the first few decades of the first century have always helped to militate against strong forces that have sought to reduce the Christian religion to ideas. In doing so, Christian thought rejects the tendency to find refuge in abstraction, of fleeing from history to the comfortable realm of the transcendent where beliefs fit firmly into tidy systems and so function as their own reward. The contingency of Christianity's central facts resists their being construed as timeless truths.[42] Yet, exactly because of this, we can see how theology shares Nietzsche's incentive, *mutatis mutandis*, for adopting an aphoristic style. Counter-intuitively to be sure, the appearance of timelessness that aphorism has is yet merely an appearance. Rather than *defining* the knowledge to which it seems to refer, it actually chastens the sweep of its own ability to define, limiting itself to make room for the reader's meaning. But its limiting function is matched with its continual suggestion of *more*, that there is a meaning that lies beyond it that exceeds it. It happens that this is an apt description of Christian knowledge.

Nietzsche especially disliked the doctrinaire Christianity that was a part of his nineteenth-century German experience.[43] Rigid formulae only indicate, at best, how unhelpful doctrine becomes for life and, at worst, how it positively destroys life. Once the attitudinal, affective aspect disappears, only bald propositions are left. As before, his dissatisfaction has its origins in the failure of any doctrine to correspond to the nature of reality as constantly in flux. The fullness of a lived life requires a light touch ill-afforded by anything characterized by everlasting conditions suited to timeless circumstances which, as historic beings, we must know do not really exist.[44] As Zarathustra continuously exhorted those who would listen, "be true to the earth!"[45]

In affirming the reality of flux for its own very different reasons,[46] Christian thought has only in some strains attempted to avoid doctrine altogether. When present, a suspicion of creeds typically makes appeals to the irreducibly historic character of Christian existence together with an affirmation of the spontaneous work of the Holy Spirit. But in the main, theology has not imagined that, in doctrine, it was being unhistorical.[47] Some recent theologians like George Lindbeck intend precisely to give a narrative account of doctrine, showing that there is a context to doctrinal formulations both in how they have been produced and in how they are preserved throughout time by the church.[48] The origins of doctrinal statements, of course, themselves occur within time and give expression to particular ways that Christian forebears reasoned, how they read and discerned the Scriptures, and how they worshipped in their time and in response to historical pressures. Subsequent generations then seek to sustain these developments by continuing to reinhabit them in their confessions, within the ongoing life of the church's narrative that it both tells and inhabits as time advances. On this account, what the church affirms is therefore not revealed in a way anterior to its real history, as in Euripides' Prologues, but is temporally always a matter of suspense—or, better, of promise and trust.

To be sure, Nietzsche would not have wanted to think of Christian belief in this way. But his critiques of dogmatism, once orthodox belief has been purged of historical development, parallel what Christian thought, at its best, has always affirmed. "It is the sure sign of the death of a religion when its mythic presuppositions become systematized, under the severe, rational eyes of an orthodox dogmatism into a ready sum of historical events."[49] Put differently, when history becomes objectified, it serves a non-historical purpose like the Prologue and Epilogue that narrate future and past events at a temporal remove from their actual occurrence. The challenge for Christian thought has likewise been to inhabit its confessions *as confessions* that are made in the present tense. These are to make reference to the present constitution of the church and its chief characteristics in such a way that it is not easy to relegate such pronouncements only to the past or the future. Doing so inevitably mitigates present churchly life of the risks and uncertainties that attend to confessing these things *now* while waiting on God's promises for what the future may hold for a people who so confess.[50]

An example is the church's confession that it is the Body of Christ. This confession is made in the present tense in such a way that, in its confessing, the Body of Christ is actually formed as a confessing body. This means simply that the presence of the Body of Christ in the world cannot be identified except insofar as there are people who claim that this identity is decidedly *theirs* with the attendant recognition that this is an identity that is greater than the sum of its parts precisely due to the present risen life of Christ. The uncertainty of the full extent or complete grasp of what is being confessed is, therefore, actually part of the truth of that confession. If the knowledge of what constitutes Christian iden-tity as the Body of Christ were exhaustible, in other words, then it could not be a true confession. In this respect, it is important that the church is, in Robert Jenson's apt phrase, a "historically continuous community" whose existence is actually part of the content of its speech when it proclaims the gospel and produces theological work.[51] That such a community is not separable from its products necessarily means that what it produces can be no less historic. Nevertheless, its products are not permitted to pass into irrelevance so long as they continue to exist as part of the mem-ory of the church (at the least) and the constitutive practice of the church's enduring presence in the world (at the most).

By now, of course, we have left Nietzsche behind in many sig-nificant respects. Yet his crucial insight concerning the self-involving nature of tragedy (and the present meaningfulness of aphorism) crucially paves the way for Christian appropriation and articulation. Just as the Greek chorus most effectively serves the connection between the performance and life when it refuses a purely didactic role—which Nietzsche characterizes as rationalistic—so also the story Christians tell must be more than information if it is to be true. For example, Herbert McCabe is right to point out that the Christian claim that we are loved by God is not known or shared as a piece of information or a proposition that submits to efforts at verifying it, but that what is communicated to us is nothing less than the very fact of our being loved.[52] This may admittedly sound like a subtle distinction, and perhaps its subtlety is an artifact of modern epistemology's triumph. Still, there is something dramatic about the ease with which God's love seems to convert to theory without remainder in an idiom where truth is more readily associated with information than with love.

It is possible, of course, to reflect further in a number of different ways on these themes. Nietzsche's own proclivity for the aphorism and the parable (which is really a modified, extended aphorism) suggests itself for considering the parables of Jesus in this light.[53] They represent and indicate knowledge without directly pointing to it, obliquely indicating something beyond the literal words of the story being told. In this way, they stand as invitations to the hearer to include herself in its narrative, which is why Jesus's explanation as to the purpose of parables can be so mystifying: "for those outside everything is in parables; so that they may indeed see but not perceive, and may indeed hear but not understand; lest they should turn again, and be forgiven."[54] Mark tells of five instances of Jesus calling people and at least eleven of him telling people to go away. On one level, Nietzsche's Zarathustra, who is so obviously Jesus-like, is in the same position when his calling of disciples is almost entirely met with disbelief and misunderstanding. It is not as though the meaning of his speeches is opaque, but that the speeches fail to convince the unbelievers exactly inasmuch as the unbelievers persist in their unbelief. And even though Nietzsche later chastised Christian faith for being out of touch with reality compared to science,[55] the posture of his Zarathustra is nearer the mark: the reality of a people unprepared for a radical message—whether the death of God and the impending arrival of the *Übermensch* or else the kingdom of God—are in no position for the truth of the message to become their knowledge so long as they stand on the outside. The New Testament parables function to sift people—those who have ears to hear from those who do not. Jesus does not call everyone to follow him, not everyone he calls follows, and some want to follow but he sends them away—often because their response in faith is enough.

However, what is crucial is that parables do not make an argument. There is no necessary connection between the information contained in the story and the story's effect in making a disciple. As both fictions and narratives, parables are not easily refutable. How does one refute a story, particularly one whose truth does not pretend to rely on the rightness of historical facts? "A sower went out to sow" is not a historical claim, nor is "A man was going down from Jerusalem to Jericho, and he fell among robbers." And yet the truth of the stories is also not to be found at the level of the timeless truth, though they can have the appearance of tending toward reductive admonitions such as "show compassion to your enemies." However, parables resist being boiled down in this way because what they accomplish in terms of sifting the hearers (good soil versus rocky soil, for example) cannot be accomplished apart from the story itself. In this way, parables realize more effectively, what Nietzsche hoped from his aphorisms and, indeed, when he finally abandons the aphorism, it is immediately replaced by the parables of Zarathustra.[56]

In addition to Zarathustra being Jesus-like, he is also set within a larger work that is itself an enormous parable, making the speaker of parables a kind of narrator of the literary aim of the whole text. Likewise, the parables of Jesus are clues to readers with "ears to hear" that Mark's Gospel is itself also a parable sown amidst a multitude of soils. This indicates that any argument being made is both on the level of the story (such as The Good Samaritan) and on the level of the whole text (Mark, Luke). This is clearly a non-standard way of making an argument, but it is exactly what Nietzsche is doing, which explains why the definitive refutation of God or anything else that is only established by a story can only be made in the form of another story. The other story will certainly be judged *better* by those convinced by it, but their being convinced can never be reduced to a single argument (or even many) propounded within it since the story itself is a kind of argument for those who would believe.

In all of this, parables represent an association with knowledge that resists grasping. The danger was not so much that any given parable would be misunderstood, but that they would indeed be understood by the wrong people, accepted out of season by pot-lookers.[57] And this is not only true of the *form* of parables as parables but is actually also a theme common to many of them in their content. Expectation and waiting, *not* knowing, trusting, going to sleep, rising, and wondering where the bounteous crop came from: these are frequently what the parables are about. We are tempted to say that they are the *point* of some parables except that reducing a story to a point or core is too quick a hermeneutical move, one that can jeopardize the very function of the story to aid in curbing anticipation. Von Balthasar sees the theme of patience throughout the New Testament as taking priority even over humility. Indeed, the sin is characterized as the attempt to break out of time, to know the Father's will in advance, something Jesus himself especially resists.[58]

The ethically decisive aim of *The Birth of Tragedy* may be summarized by the insight that humanity can never tell stories that are grander than our own participation in them. As potential interpreters of others' stories, we are drawn in and asked to declare how things look from within them. Nietzsche thus diagnoses the proclivity for human cultures to believe lies, particularly concerning human importance. But the storytelling function is subject to its own perversions. If we sin by standing at a distance, we may also perpetuate another kind of falsehood through participation in a story we believe and declare to be true. In his famous early essay, "On Truth and Lies in the Nonmoral Sense," Nietzsche accounts for our habit of calling some things true, not due to their being true or else having a particular property ("Are designations congruent with things? [No!]"[59]), but only due to sheer convention: we call those things true that we *agree* to call true.[60] Then, crucially, we conveniently forget that we have reached this linguistic consensus—in fact, we *need* to forget to allow our confidence in the language we have agreed upon to exercise its full effect. And since the material content of these "truths" function to elevate a culture's self-importance (or even that of the whole race), the rise of truth likewise suggests that humanity ought to undergo an appropriate mortification.

> Once upon a time, in some out of the way corner of that universe which is dispersed into numberless twinkling solar systems, there was a star upon which clever beasts invented knowing. That was the most arrogant and mendacious minute of "world history," but nevertheless, it was only a minute. After nature had drawn a few breaths, the star cooled and congealed, and the clever beasts had to die.[61]

If we ever believed that our status was more important than this—less fleeting, more central to the way things are—then we have only deceived ourselves. Our palliative maneuvers have yielded grandiose theories and expedient speech. "We believe that we know something about the things themselves when we speak of trees, colors, snow, and flowers; and yet we possess nothing but metaphors for things—metaphors which correspond in no way to the original entities." And our verbal claims to truth are only the deployment of the "usual metaphors."

This early essay is notorious for seeming to say not only that those things we call true are not true after all, but apparently much worse, that they are actually lies, and doubly so. They are first lies because they parade themselves as true (and the parading is itself a form of deception) and second because we conspire to keep their true nature (metaphors) hidden.

However, an objection might be raised. Just because we agree to call some things true does not necessarily mean that they are not true.[62] It only means that they cannot be true *simply* because we call them true. There is a fallacy in this syllogism:

> There are many kinds of eyes. Even the sphinx has eyes— and consequently there are many kinds of "truths," and consequently there is no truth.[63]

We might call the fallacy the automatic movement from pluralism to relativism (see Chapter 6). When Nietzsche says that the metaphors we use "correspond in no way to the original entities," is he making a linguistic point about the limits of language or a psychological point about the extent of our self-deception? In this regard, some have claimed that Nietzsche's account in this essay is actually much more mundane than has often been believed. In a mild form, it amounts to a kind of perspectivism that preserves the Kantian distinction between essences and appearances we noticed earlier. The common failure all of our linguistic attempts at expressing truth share, then, is intrinsic in the fact that every account expresses a different point of view. It is a failure to correspond to original entities rather than the denial of original entities themselves.

So far, we have been conflating Nietzsche's rejection of metaphysics with his denial of truth. The nature of their connection is a matter of some debate, particularly as it seems that Nietzsche modified his positions relative to them over time. Maudemarie Clark argues that Nietzsche's early position is contradictory, in which he denies all truth even though it obviously must be the case that a denial of any sort aims at being true, otherwise there would be no difference between denying and affirming something. Nevertheless, Clark does not think this is finally the position Nietzsche wants to defend in his mature works (she says, after *BGE*). The early Nietzsche of *BT* and "On Truth and Lies in the Non-moral Sense" was not able to differentiate between metaphysical truth and truth so long as he remained committed to a theory of truth that he will later come to reject, namely, that all truth is metaphysical through correspondence to things in themselves.[64] The curiosity for Nietzsche's early works, therefore, is not as much his brazen denial of truth ("Truths are illusions which we have forgotten are illusions"[65]) as it is his persistence in holding a Kantian metaphysics. What he really wanted to deny, in other words, was not truth, but a particular theory of truth (correspondence) that looked like "truth" so long as it was taken to be the only such theory. We may therefore observe an irony, given Nietzsche's frequent trope of truth as illusion: that the illusion which prevented Nietzsche from thinking alternatives to correspondence was taken to be true even while he knew he needed to reject it and with it, truth itself. Nietzsche would not have reached this incoherent point if he had more straightforwardly conceived of truth free from the illusion of theory. Clark argues that in his final two years,

Nietzsche realized that if his rejection of the thing-in-itself is thoroughgoing, there is no basis for denying truth.[66] But until then, he continued to assert parallel rejections of both metaphysics and truth, assuming the former includes the latter.

Nietzsche's later phase is more explicitly genealogical and seemingly the possibility of its being true is crucial to the success of any genealogy. There is little use in putting forward a genealogical analysis of a system of power, say, if that analysis is simply one possible interpretation among many. In *Genealogy of Morals*, for example, Nietzsche narrates the mythic origins of Christian morality and his myth needs to be true to keep from being indicted for merely asserting the pagan point of view which Christian morality supplanted.[67] If his myth were not true, then there would be nothing to differentiate the *ressentiment* he pins on slave morality from his own narratival attempt to do battle against that morality. Therefore, Nietzsche needs truth in his explicitly genealogical phase; yet he does not just separate truth from metaphysics for the convenience of making his own position more credible. Instead, genealogy is meant to stand in an entirely different relation to truth than did the versions that relied on metaphysical correspondence. This means that genealogy makes no *appeal* to anything other than its own story; it is not persuasive *because* it can be proven true on any other grounds. This makes genealogy at once both powerful and vulnerable.

The power of genealogy lies in its appeal to *intuition*. The genealogy's truth is vastly different from the truth of the syllogism. The former makes use of lyric force rather than direct refutation to sideline objections. Nietzsche boasts that he writes in blood, with enormous depth of feeling, deeper than the logicians—and this is how he claimed to live his life.[68] This passion encounters the reader so baldly that one is often inclined, as with the truth of aphoristic statements, either to take him or leave him rather than weigh his reasoning. To be sure, Nietzsche himself reasoned, often quite carefully. But he had no desire to win converts through reasoning, but rather through intuition: "If a person could not see what he saw, Nietzsche would not convert him by argument."[69] If the truth could not be seen intuitively, it must not be worth pursuing.

Nevertheless, genealogy is also vulnerable precisely in its dependence on lyricism. To Nietzsche, philosophy is more akin to music than to mathematics and physics and it therefore calls for artists to employ their craft with consummate skill.[70] The stakes are exceedingly high. After all, if one's practiced craft does not elicit an intuitive response, how would one know whether the failure was a failure of the craft or simply an intellectually dim audience? As an argument, genealogy is not concluded when it exists in a written form like a scientific formula. Instead, it is alive in every encounter where its force is tested according to whether the force of the encounter is appropriate to the object of knowledge.

In some respects, we might say that this exhibits an extraordinary trust in the power of both truth and art. Yet the trust in truth's power is only a way of restating the power of the art since where the art of capturing the imagination is absent, any question of truth is moot. This is another sense in which Nietzsche rejects correspondence theories. Language does not correspond to any more fundamental truth since there is nothing beyond the lyric power of language. The question of whether or not it persuades will need to be observed in practice—whether it *actually* persuades in this setting as opposed to that. But then does Nietzsche simply reduce truth to persuasion and therefore to power? The exigency of this question becomes clearer in Nietzsche's later works: it is not that the truth *requires* lyrical power to be believed; it is that the truth itself *is* power, appealing as it does to the will rather than to the intellect. The appeal of this Dionysian wisdom is continuous with Nietzsche's later and all-encompassing notion of the will to power.[71]

Nietzsche claimed to philosophize with a hammer to sound out idols.[72] If aphorism sets the hammer against conventional scholarly discourse by appealing to meaning in a non-standard sense, Nietzsche's mature attempts are even more devastating, if perhaps finally impossible: the complete abandonment of the use of statements to convey *anything* beyond the present play of statements. In the end, what Nietzsche wants to say, comments Alasdair MacIntyre, "cannot be expressed as a set of statements." MacIntyre continues:

> Statements are made only to be discarded—and sometimes
> taken up again—in that movement from utterance
> to utterance in which what is communicated is

the movement. Nietzsche did not advance a new theory against older theories; he proposed an abandonment of theory.[73]

For this reason, it seems certain that interpreters are expressing an inordinate devotion to analytical thought when they insist that, for all his invectives, Nietzsche still needs logic and the fixed elements of discourse, or even (as noted above) that he needs a concept of truth in his genealogical phase.[74] After all, in wielding a hammer, genealogies do not need to be *true*, they just need to *win*.[75] Even scientists, Nietzsche exposes, are moralists exactly inso-far as they revel in the truth of their conclusions *as the direct outcomes of their scientific efforts*—their truths somehow being accounted as better and of greater value than others owing to their having been arrived at through scientific means.[76] But if the amount (and style) of effort is immaterial to the value of truth, then there can exist no necessary connection between the rigor of the argument and the truth of its conclusion. Alternatively, the argument may have inter-nal value, included in which is the logical conclusion, but this simply says nothing about the truth reached; it just wins.[77]

It is wide of the mark to blame Socrates for all of this, of course, even while he is emblematic of more recent difficulties. The Socratic corruption of the Dionysian spirit is the inverse of what is taking place in the modern era. In Nietzsche's own time, he observed what he took to be the beginning of the end of a failed scientific and rationalistic project: "Socratic man has run his course."[78] A change of recovery was afoot in Germany, a move-ment occurring within a listless culture of degradation that masked its lack of depth through hard work. Nietzsche saw an enormous opportunity for the rebirth of Greek culture's greatness, of art that had long been stifled through dry academic logic. Nietzsche strik-ingly exhorts his readers to embrace this opportunity:

> Indeed, my friends, believe with me in this Dionysian life and in the rebirth of tragedy! . . . Dare to lead the life of tragic man, and you will be redeemed. It has fallen to your lot to lead the Dionysian procession out of India into Greece. Gird yourselves for a severe conflict, but have faith in the thaumaturgy of your god![79]

To be sure, Nietzsche did not intend for his polemic to be restricted to eulogizing one period of Greek Theater over another. What he provides in *The Birth of Tragedy* is nothing less than a historical resemblance with what he sees as a thoroughly *modern* dilemma, which explains his reference to Descartes. But if it is the case that Descartes himself—the supreme rationalist in the history of modern philosophy—appeals to divine trustworthiness to substantiate convictions that we share about the reality of what is disclosed to us, then Nietzsche must conclude that this rationalism is actually deeply superstitious. It purports to respect only cold rationality but is acutely steeped in metaphysical accounts of reality that may or may not be rational, but either way surely do not accord with the mode of rationality Descartes himself advanced. For Nietzsche, this must mean that "rational" too is a form of subterfuge, a deceptive way of talking about knowledge that still grounds itself in metaphysics. In Chapter 6, we will consider how Nietzsche's own metaphysical accounts fare against those he opposes.

If Christianity has no particular stake in the idea of truth, truth-as-such, or in defending theories of truth, it is for reasons that Nietzsche helps theology to articulate. The irreducible particularity of Christian truth is perhaps a scandal in every age, but as Saint Paul says, it is "folly to the Greeks" and precisely by way of Nietzsche's identification of Socrates' self-imposed account of what may pass for knowledge and therefore truth.[80] The transmission of Christian truth cannot be reduced to a list of beliefs or propositions about the nature of reality but must come to every setting as a story—which is only to say as a gospel. Meanwhile, the modern suspicion of any such accounts that cannot submit to its two-stage epistemology will simply have to content itself with an exaltation of its own theories, its limited because *a priori* systems, and ultimately, its tiny gods.

Chapter 3

Culture of nothingness

Two key aspects of Nietzsche's thought run parallel to each other: his critique of the way that history is used and abused, and his inter-related doctrines of the Eternal Recurrence and the *Übermensch*. These aspects complement each other, the former dealing with the past and the present, the latter with the future. The former pronounces a definitive "No" to the ways that Nietzsche saw his culture telling the past in a way that allowed them also to remain relatively unchanged in the future. The latter is an affirmative "Yes", a recommendation for a future for which we can make no excuses nor avoid the responsibility of striving toward it. The present chapter takes up Nietzsche's attack on history while the following chapter focuses on Nietzsche's positive teaching of both the Eternal Recurrence and the *Übermensch*.

Nietzsche's century was impressed with progress and narrated it through an ever-bright future made possible by commitments to materialism, realism, and scientism. The Enlightenment had already cleared the cobwebs from the medieval mind; now the culture was advancing with the material fruits of an intellectual housecleaning through a technological renaissance. The historical consciousness of Nietzsche's day was a form of optimism.

> These historical men believe that the meaning of existence will come more and more to light in the course of its *process*, and they glance behind them only so that . . . they can learn to understand the present and to desire the future more vehemently.[1]

An optimistic approach to the future involves bearing preju-dice against the past. If the past is *for* the future, as optimism holds, then history exists for the sake of an education that can only be true to the past so long as the past is incomplete, awaiting fulfillment through some future consummation. Yet, Nietzsche thinks, if the past only finds meaning in the future, we must surely conclude the same about the present. There can be nothing that present existence holds that will not at some future time be augmented and enhanced through hindsight. Such futures are continually deferred since each subsequent future then provides a greater vantage than the ones that came before. But Nietzsche acknowledges that life is always lived in the present, meaning that if life is to be enhanced rather than diminished, a different sort of character from the "historical man" must emerge, namely, the suprahistorical man,

> who sees no salvation in the process and for whom, rather, the world is complete and reaches its finality at each and every moment. What could ten more years teach that the past ten were unable to teach! . . . [T]he past and the present are one.[2]

The past and the present coinhere in that they are not pulled apart by a future that sits in judgment over every historical moment.

Moreover, the nineteenth century was characterized by a realism that Nietzsche might have applauded given its unremitting determination to take reality as it is, to disclaim all of those pretensions and prejudices that gratuitously parade themselves as features of the world firmly within the knower's unmediated clutch. But the realism against which Nietzsche reacted was just a newer façade. It made appeals to science to achieve a reduction of all things to their most basic parts, an approach that always comes at a great cost, depriving things of their function within realms larger than themselves. This radical separation of one thing from another is only a version of the tendency to detach the facts of history from the people and culture that constitute that history, craving the possession of historical products as discrete fragments that are easily accommodated within a contemporary milieu, ultimately owing nothing to the past after all. Even though it spoke the language of realism, German culture in Nietzsche's century betrayed its own decrees by recruiting the real in a project of cultural control and renovation. A true realism can never sit easily with assurances of optimism insofar as realism accepts the contingency of existence; tragedy is the true realism.

Together with the flamboyant composer Richard Wagner, Nietzsche worried that European culture in the nineteenth century was really just an empty shell. It lacked the power of myth for enriching social and cultural life, something that religion had previously provided, of course; but Christian Europe had yet to come to terms with the cultural consequences of the fact that it had jettisoned Christianity. In its place, it attempted to make the most of its newfound treasures: technology, rationalization, and a mechanical approach to nature (like a wind-up clock) and morality (the formulae of utilitarianism). Romanticism had been attempting to overcome the strictures of the Enlightenment by attending to the emotional side of knowledge, but its wonder before the inexpressibilities of life had not won the day after all, yielding finally to the industrial mindset. Scientific reduction had certainly not spared the mythological.

Even the noblest attempts of the industrial spirit at culture were only thinly interesting veneers. The industrial spirit yielded seemingly endless productivity, keeping whole nations busy with work, establishing the conditions that would elicit Marx's legendary analysis. Control of nature and control of history coincide in the positivist disassembly of parts from whole in the optimistic discovery of veiled secrets, of fundamental essences. But as subjects of a controlling present, history's facts bend to contemporary configurations that serve the primary function of congratulating the present for its superiority over what came before. This, for Nietzsche, is the abuse of history for life, the subject of one of his *Untimely Meditations*. The past is judged in terms of the present, exalting the present as more advanced; meanwhile, the present is seen in continuity with what is great about *its* past, not least is the fact that it has a past that, despite everything else, is strong and established. As such, any culture that makes use of the past in this way cannot help being a culture that encourages self-deception, allowing those who are its champions to be satisfied with tenuous (though academically sanctioned) connections to a glorious, classical past. History, like the work that attends to it, distracts people from life's emptiness, the confusion about who we are and what we ought to be doing. Numbed through ceaseless recall, the historical consciousness forgets to live now. Recycling history creates work for the recyclers, but there is little left over for genuine use of the recycled products. This is, as Nietzsche saw, by design since the nature of the appeals to the past, the tools and techniques employed, preclude authentic life.

> But it is sick, this unchained life, and needs to be cured.
> It is sick with many illnesses and not only with the mem-
> ory of its chains—what chiefly concerns us here is that it is
> suffering from the *malady of history*. Excess of history has
> attacked life's plastic powers, it no longer knows how to
> employ the past as a nourishing food.[3]

Nietzsche adduced that this abuse could only be salvaged through an exact and drastic inversion. Where we are tempted to ascertain our superiority based on our reading of history, we ought to doubt that we have read the history rightly and attend more closely to it. Nietzsche's own exaltation of Greek culture attempts this inversion in that the exaltation is itself a critique of modernity. At the same time, when there now appears nowhere to go, no direction that presents itself more compellingly over others, a culture ought to strike out in blithe indifference to its past if that past is of little help. In this way, Nietzsche insists that we actively create the past by living in the present (since all past was once present). Greek culture did not create a noble past for those who would come after them by considering their own legacy. Like modern culture, the Greeks were beset with dangers of being overcome by what was past and foreign, "of perishing through 'history'."

> They never lived in proud inviolability: their "culture" was,
> rather, for a long time a chaos of foreign, Semitic,
> Babylonian, Lydian, Egyptian forms and ideas, and their
> religion truly a battle of all the gods of the East: somewhat
> as "German culture" and religion is now a struggling chaos
> of all the West and of all past ages.[4]

The superiority of the Greeks, however, was evident in their determination to advance culturally in spite of all of these forces. They learned to "organize the chaos" by devoting themselves to the Delphic Oracle's teaching to "know thyself," which Nietzsche observes with Heraclitus is not the dispensation of a knowledge, but only exists as an indication and an invitation, an empty space that must be filled by that which is much more than knowledge: one's very existence. This is the perennial challenge to culture in which the Greeks prevailed.

The Greeks seized responsibility for their own destiny in such a way that their greatness lay precisely in not giving thought to their legacy but only to the nobility of their present life. They discovered how to enhance and augment those things to which they had become heirs, overcoming and superseding them, becoming, in Nietzsche's nomenclature, "supra-historical." What then is more true to the Greek past? Is it to feign antiquity, staging fake battles, and dressing up the present in old-fashioned ornaments, as Nietzsche accuses his contemporaries? Or is it to become in some measure like the Greeks themselves, including in their very disregard of history? For the latter, a culture must seize its own vitality in the realization that the past is always dead and so, ironically, that culture will only be true to its history when it has acquired the skill for knowing when to ignore it.[5]

In place of failed modern culture, Wagner proposed the mythic subject matter of his operas along with their operatic form as myth's great artistic expression. Because modernity failed to describe itself in mythic terms, Wagner reasoned, it could not help but produce substandard art. Rescuing Europe from the ruin of Christianity and its subsequent effects on culture, therefore, would come from nothing less than an artistic rebirth. According to Wagner, it is not necessary to envision a state of existence beyond the artistic one, which is for him life's highest form. Art takes the place of religion, with myths underwriting a humanistic doctrine of salvation: what shall we do if the gods are incompetent to save? The myth of the heroic, liberated, strong individual functions religiously for Wagner. But for Nietzsche, art must serve life and so it cannot be an end in itself. Even though music and art are exalted pursuits, they are exalted only through their close approximation to life. Wagner and Nietzsche both sought better art through new and revived myths, even while Nietzsche was later to become dissatisfied with what he took to be Wagner's complacency, his settling for a religious role for myth that ultimately fails to overcome what Nietzsche took to be abhorrent about religion. Myth continued to provide the comfort that religion no longer could. Yet did that not condemn it exactly to a religious function? Does it not yield a "merely decorative culture" that Nietzsche assumed must be a casualty of the rise of *true* culture?[6]

Nietzsche notoriously problematized distinctions between those things that we comfortably call moral and those we call amoral or morally neutral. It is important to see how Nietzsche's critiques of history are actually critiques of the morality surrounding history, how history is always already bound up with the moral questions of *use* and *abuse*. In the indomitable words of Nietzsche's contemporary, Julius Langbehn, in a letter to a friend, "I shall now cease to study the past, instead I shall *construct the future*."[7] And this is a decidedly *moral* determination that is thoroughly Nietzschean in inspiration. The goal of humanity is no longer temporal, the becoming of a world-process, as the philosophy of the day described it or as the Last Judgment had promised. "No," Nietzsche wrote, "the goal of humanity cannot lie in its end but only in its highest exemplars."[8] The meaning of history is not embedded within the historical process, to be made evident in the future; instead, it is itself the great cultured few that a culture's determined felicity with its own history will in time produce. In later writings, these few are given the name *Übermensch*.

Nevertheless, it would be a mistake to assume that Nietzsche is critical of history's *content*. Such critique would surely be a hopeless project since the events of history are contingent, that is, they are some ways but might have been otherwise. As such, they do not answer to any standard and so are exempt from critique. They are not, of course, exempt from the kind of *moral* critique in which some things in the past can be assessed as being horrible. But they are only exempt in the sense that the events of history cannot be construed as somehow evincing a greater cumulative meaning or otherwise faulted for failing to do so. The question is therefore one of the interpretation of contingent events. On the one hand, this gives rise to questions about history's events as clusters around the direction and goal history might be taken to imply, where discrete happenings are more bearable when incorporated into a larger narrative or progression, that is, decorative myth. On the other hand are questions about what makes an event a discrete event in the first place: When should the story of one event begin and when should it end? Isolating too many happenings, separating them from what goes before them and what follows from them may falsely objectify things and, ironically, as a procedure may suggest its own recourse to conditions or givens for defining one event as "an event" and not a part of another.

One way this kind of interpretation is carried out practically is by the efforts of a culture to make a past *mean something* for the present. Often the past in question is *their* past, the people who settled here as opposed to there, who produced this culture as opposed to that. But this is not always the case; for example, every Western culture seems to fancy itself as ancestors of the Greeks. The determinations necessary to know whether history's content is well suited (rather than destructive) to the activity of the present will always depend on a genuine assessment of those actions that the present requires. But Nietzsche argues that our ability to know what should be done is already a function of putting a certain amount of critical distance between ourselves and our pasts (or our culture and our culture's past). This distance is achieved through forgetting what has gone before, at least to the extent that the shadow the past casts over the present does not exhaustively determine the present.[9]

The erudite historians Nietzsche critiques simply wanted the wrong kind of distance. Theirs was the kind of detachment that comes from knowledge of the past coupled with a historical consciousness that sanctioned resignation to inevitability. A focus on learning and dwelling on history can become an excuse for inaction. Nietzsche's esteem for Hellenic thought and culture did not only lead him to acknowledge the inapt treatment that that culture and time too often occasioned as being antithetical to Greek particularities. It also led him to suspect that, insofar as *all* history recounts actions, there can be no true action of remembrance that is not itself, in some major respect, an *enacted* past. I have already noted Nietzsche's dissatisfaction with philosophers who give priority to non-historical concepts, elevating them over historical ones.[10] This may seem like a contradiction given the scholarly fascination with the past, seemingly releasing historians from the critique leveled at philosophers in this regard. But Nietzsche castigates the historical interest as well, exposing how it fails to be true to its object so long as the scholars persist in rendering the past *safe* for modern consumption precisely by de-historicizing it. Nietzsche likens them to worshippers of Egyptian mummies, making idols tame for their veneration, killing and stuffing historical concepts that now function as lifeless trophies.

Nietzsche's query to the historical consciousness also stimulates Christian thought from its torpor, challenging it to supply a more satisfactory account of remembrance. What, then, does it mean to *enact* memory? Remembrance is itself already a kind of act, though it may not make demands so long as it is possible to remember in a way that preserves distance from the thing remembered. The object of remembrance, after all, is not actually the past, but memories, particular ways of construing the past that highlight some things and bypass others. Remembering is therefore as much about forgetting insofar as it is not identical with reliving the past in every detail. The memory of something painful is itself also a source of pain, though not in the same way or to the same degree. We remember the experience of pain in addition to reexperiencing the pain itself, which suggests that no feeling can be fully accommodated within the memory. Nietzsche argues that we can live neither without memory nor without forgetting. The cattle, he famously surmises, do in fact live without memory, in strict and constant forgetfulness of the past, giving them enviable happiness. But the human animal could never be content with the confused absence of identity in which he appeals to no past; the human being cannot be unhistorical. And this is only to say that culture (a people with a past, those who share the burden of remem-brance) is an irreducible part of what it is to be human. As such, we are included within culture through a determination to enlist cultural memory in the exercise of the present. The present is made, constructed, lived; it is neither given by the past nor discon-nected from it.

It seems to me that there is clearly something sacramental about Nietzsche's logic. A sacrament refers precisely through an action that simultaneously *points to* and *is* what it points to without merely pointing to itself. Signs, like past realities that are reenacted as they are remembered, participate in the reality of the things that they represent. They may also be morally formative in their reen-actment, which is to say that they form the will and shape desire.

Going further, we may adduce that the Eucharist is, just so, a sacrament of memory as an action. Quite apart from the Reformation-era debates about the real presence of Christ, it must still be crucial that the Eucharist does not *just* remember the death of Christ since something occurs in its act of remembrance beyond merely calling to mind events of the past. On the one hand, insofar as it is an action that is performed, it can never be spoken of as simply a remembrance, by which we would be made to think only about something the mind does, much like forgetting something is not properly speaking an action. Yet there is also a more central theological concern: if God raised Christ from the dead, Christ cannot merely be *remembered* in any respect by a people who claim to be constituted by Christ in the present. Consigning Christ to the past is only an aspect of recalling the existence of the church as the product of a historical occurrence, which is to say that as such its present constitution owes nothing to the Spirit of the risen Christ.[11]

To speak about the church this way is merely to adopt Nietzsche's account of how a culture ought to relate to the past. As morally formative, celebrating the Eucharist is the site of a distinctive Christian education in rightly remembering the past. The Christian learns that there is not a direct connection between the wrongs of the past and the nature of present identity even while it is mistaken to think that there is no connection between the past and the present. The intervening promise invokes the reality of transformation that is enacted anew even while it is remembered continually and repeatedly. The eucharistic elements are taken up and mysteriously transformed into the Body of Christ so that those who consume them are constituted in a new identity *as* the Body of Christ. But the elements are also continuous with the people who consume them, meaning that there are not two bodies—one in the Eucharist and one in the church—but one. Historical distance is not closed by the mind but is sacramentally traversed by the Spirit that makes the past present. A people formed by recalling a common story will partly advance the nature of their life together by being supplied with a reminder of the narrative context of their future actions. But if it were *only* this, it would still be subject to Nietzsche's critique just as much as any other people owe their identity (however insufficient or problematic, we should add) to a common story or set of stories. Thus, the church is only the church insofar as it is eucharistic; the Eucharist is only the Body of Christ when it is shared by the church. In this respect, a simple delineation cannot be made with respect to whether the church makes the Eucharist or vice versa precisely because it is both. The gestures and other actions of the priest in the Eucharist recall, for example, Christ's arms spread on the cross for those who gather in worship.[12] But, as part of the sacrament, these actions also enact what they recall. They do not point to themselves, but point to Christ, though only by way of the connection the gathered church makes within its collective memory. The movements of the priest will be utterly meaningless apart from a people whose memories are formed according to the liturgical story it tells and precisely for which it exists to tell and retell.

Of course, these very actions are also constitutive of that people insofar as they are made into the Body of Christ in the breaking of the bread. These people of memory do not pre-exist the broken bread, but their gathering around the bread-breaking is itself a function of the power of God they discover over and over again in the sacrifice of Christ—their discovery is continuous with their memory. This points to another aspect of the Eucharist's sacramental memory, namely, that both the memory of the church and the church's eucharistic performance are gifts to the church by God. The people of God not only gather in worship to celebrate the goodness of God, to enact their thanks for his grace but also to receive the grace to thank and the gifts to praise, that is, to return to God the gift of the Son by whom the church is constituted as the Body of Christ. Just as Nietzsche could not bear a fascination with history that one-sidedly served the inquirer, the eucharistic feast is reciprocal; there can be no inquirers standing at a distance, racked with an importunate desire for something that is ultimately and decisively refused.[13]

Moreover, the Eucharist is infinitely creative and mystical, that is, full of promise and possibilities always insufficiently accounted for under the rubric of memory. Prominent among the reasons for this is the claim that the Eucharist is the living Body of Christ risen. Unlike the cold mummies that furnish the intellectual closets of the philosophers for whom Nietzsche harbored so much contempt, the past of Jesus Christ can only be told truthfully in the present so long as the reality of the resurrection is not narrated as a purely historical event. It is a future-making event insofar as the resurrection's future (which includes our present) is continuously present to the risen Christ. Even so, it is not possible to capture the fullness of the resurrection within history (and certainly not within the *study* of history) exactly because the reality of the resurrection cannot simultaneously be *true* and confined to the past as the object of historical inquiry. Therefore, Nietzsche's critique of scholars who worship dead objects also applies to any theology that curbs the creativity of the living Christ even while purporting to recount Christ's history.

Sacramentally, the signs cease entirely from referring when that to which they point comes into full reality. As a sacrament of memory, the Eucharist remembers only through a simultaneous anticipation; it is not only an act of worship but also a performance of hope, a straining toward a future that will likewise be marked by worship, though in full reality of God's blessedness. Yet Nietzsche rightly suspected that a people who cannot anticipate based on their memory are bound to be disguising both the inferiority of their bond with things remembered as well as their orientation toward a brighter future. A failure to reenact the past exposes an unease within the spirit of optimism, no longer a bald march into a confident future but truly an anxious misgiving that displays as the ultimate futility of signs ever to breach the threshold of existence, however distant and far off. For Christian thought, this is the reason (as I remarked amidst introductory statements) that theology is bound to cease, to hasten its own termination; theology as a complex network of signs may refer to the sacraments (as sacramental theology obviously does) but cannot itself be sacramental except insofar as the language of theology is the language of worship, which is to say, liturgical language. But theology is always at least one step removed from liturgy, modestly taking its position subordinate to the language of worship. This makes plain that theology only has a task to achieve, a mission to discharge—indeed any content at all—so long as there are liturgical performances. Paradoxically, theology is only an intelligible exercise within a larger set of practices that delimit the complex work of churchly life, of worship and remembrance. Consequently, theology does not itself remember anything even while its legitimacy as discourse entirely depends on the practiced art of memory that likewise is authentic inasmuch as such art obviates itself through anticipating the reality of that to which it points. Theology is a discourse wholly in service to another primary mode of acting and speaking. Worship precedes and exceeds theology, precisely marking out its realm and commissioning a steady agenda of assistance. It exceeds theology by persisting in the acts theology is meant to serve, anticipating a future reality that in its very practice continues through, unmodified by the new and surprising future for which it prepares in its acts of remembrance.

The degree to which memory is also an anticipation ("For as often as you eat this bread and drink the cup, you proclaim the Lord's death until he comes"[14]) will be the extent of the memory's present enactment and reenactment. Conversely, a people with a disordered relation to the past show themselves unable to anticipate a real future that is not only continuous with the past but also, more importantly, that is reenacted in the present in any way more determinative than the mere recall of facts, terms, dates, places, events, and dead people.

There are aspects of the Eucharist that further orient those who partake of it relative to the history being recalled and enacted. The sacrament recalls and reenacts the Passion of Christ, but is not identical to it. The whole liturgical year prepares for the Passion and exaltation of Christ, centering time itself on the cross. The rhythmic concentration of the calendar on the work of Christ is recapitulated in the cadence of the Eucharist within the service of Holy Communion as it is preceded by confession, absolution, offerings, and the reconciliation of the peace and is followed by declarations, commissioning, and rejoicing in ways appropriate to the season. Steeped as it is in contingent history, the celebration resists attempts to construe it as the observance of a timeless truth (by definition, one does not need to *remember* timeless truths in the historical sense). Instead, the senses are crucially involved in a complex manner that is not obvious or immediately apparent. The Eucharist can never be anything but a *bodily* memory. Medieval formulations of transubstantiation (of which Thomas Aquinas's is only one, though the best known) attempted to correct against a "sensual" explanation of the eucharistic presence in which, so long as the faith of the recipient was great enough, the bread and wine impress on the senses the reality of flesh and blood rather than the characteristics of their unconsecrated condition. Against this, the new doctrine appealed to a metaphysical distinction from Aristotle, that between substance and accident. It affirmed that the substance changed while the accidents (taste, appearance, smell) remained the same. This change could be said to be a *real* change because what truly matters is the substance of something while accidents, as the term implies, are only incidental to a thing's identity.

It is easy to discern that this distinction is one version of an ancient and enduring separation of essence from appearance. Nietzsche criticized Plato for it and Kant for another version of it.[15] In its multifarious forms, it constitutes for Nietzsche the mistaken and self-deluding tendency of yearning to flee from the world of appearance, that is, from the world as it presents itself to our senses. In this respect, Nietzsche is to be ranked among the existentialists for whom existence precedes essence. The ancient and enduring mistake, however, originates in the confluence of the noble intention to discover the locus of true being while not being deceived about it and the base intention so quickly to disparage the senses in this discovery. "There must be some deception which prevents us from perceiving that which has being: where is the deceiver?" ask the philosophers.

> We have found him! . . . it is the senses! These senses,
> which are so immoral in other ways too, deceive us
> concerning the *true* world. Moral: let us free ourselves
> from the deception of the senses, from becoming, from
> history, from lies; history is nothing but faith in the senses,
> faith in lies. Moral: let us say No to all who have faith in
> the senses, to all the rest of mankind; they are all "mob."
> Let us be philosophers! . . . And above all, away with the
> body, this wretched *idée fixe* of the senses, disfigured
> by all the fallacies of logic, refuted, even impossible,
> although it is impudent enough to behave as if it
> were real![16]

As much as he seems to, Nietzsche does not here *primarily* fault philosophy's conclusion (in its exalted reason) that the senses are to blame for their failure to see things as they really are. Instead, he diagnoses their malevolent *propensity for blaming the senses*, their hatred of the body and its faculties with which it interfaces the sensual world, which therefore entails a hatred of the material world. This is the reason Nietzsche includes the binary opposition of reality and appearance in the many species of self-deception he enumerates. In the end, "the antithesis of the apparent world and the true world is reduced to the antithesis 'world' and 'nothing'."[17] In this way, being true to the earth is a hedge against nihilism, nothingness.

Perhaps philosophy has tended to produce brains on sticks, disembodied reasoners who resent the crass, imperceptive weight of flesh and bone for their obstruction in the pursuit of pure ideas. Christians too have proffered their own versions, where the soul is a ghostly presence within the body or, in the most severe form, the body's prisoner. Even though the Second Council of Constantinople rejected Christological formulations along these lines in AD 553, Christian antipathy toward the body has endured through the centuries, the modern period being no different. As before, Descartes exemplifies this with intensity when he writes, "I found that the distinction between things such as mind and body . . . is much greater than the distinction between things which are such that when we think of both of them we do not see how one can exist apart from the other."[18] With Nietzsche, we are right to wonder what kind of philosophy could allow Descartes to think that minds and bodies might have existences apart from each other, particularly when every philosopher has had a body.

Nietzsche, however, exempts Heraclitus from this characterization because Heraclitus opposed the tide of philosophical opinion that distrusted the senses because they revealed the world to be rough, contingent, out of harmony, and full of variation.[19] Heraclitus too distrusted the bodily senses but for the opposite reason: he thought they misleadingly showed the world to be full of stable, unified things. Nietzsche thinks Heraclitus is closer to the mark for having appreciated the true nature of things in their impermanence and lack of unity even though he was wrong to consider that the reason that we ever thought otherwise lies with sense perception. To Nietzsche, the senses are not the deceivers, but reason is. "'Reason' is the cause of our falsification of the testimony of the senses."[20] Even though the senses do not lie, it is not quite possible to say that they tell the truth since "truth" belongs to the vocabulary of reason; all that the senses can do is present to us the "apparent" world which is the only world there is. This means that the senses *cannot* lie (since they cannot tell the truth), but reason can and does lie insofar as it makes of the world anything more united and harmonious than our senses reveal *and* insofar as it accuses the senses of lying.

In claiming these things, Nietzsche styles himself as a commentator on theology. He took belief in God to be bound up with the exaltation of human reason, not primarily because he was acquainted with a rationalistic Christianity (although he was) but because reason has nearly always been construed as a divine faculty. Theology is not too philosophical; philosophy is too theological. Nevertheless, Christianity *is* too philosophical to the extent that it has appropriated the thoughts of Greece (which were shared by India, Nietzsche points out): that we must have previously been divine since we have reason. Where else could it have come from? We notice that things in the world have essence, identity, "thinghood." Rather than conclude that our reason is lying to us about this, we congratulate ourselves for having so exalted a faculty.[21] There is a *double* deception here. First, there is the deception of reason which we do not notice because, second, we are also deceiving ourselves about the status of our reason.

We must also notice how this relates to memory and recalling the past. In Nietzsche's characterization, reason *remembers* our divinity where the memory is enlisted in a move of self-deception, a perfidious grasping after mythic origins that assists us in singing our own praises, revealing our penchant for idolatry and self-fascination. Moreover, remembering is here a work of the reasoning faculty and as such, we might say it is *too interested* in remembering a particularly self-aggrandizing past for itself (and not just for ourselves as reasoners). In this regard, eucharistic remembering resists idolatry. If reason remembers our divinity, the Eucharist remembers Christ's humanity. The difference is twofold: first, eucharistic memory is enacted, making any attempt to understand *that* faculty's origin only a push closer to the incarnate Christ who was physically like us; second, as a mystery, it certainly ceases to be an authentic practice when it is exclusively captured by reason.

Still, Nietzsche thought that the ascendancy of science in his day was evidence that this trend (brains on sticks) was being reversed, that the testimony of the senses was being accepted. But in the century since Nietzsche, philosophy too has witnessed a variety of attempts to take seriously our embodiment as a datum for thinking.[22] In approaching history through the Eucharist, we are not interrogating the embodied nature of knowledge (historical or otherwise) only *as such* since, as a strategy, this cannot help but reproduce some of the inadequacies from which we must attempt to distance ourselves when traveling alongside Nietzsche. Instead, the question of the sensual nature of the eucharistic feast is already a concrete, historically embodied inquiry. The inquiry may press for manifold details: What is the nature of the Christian encounter with the past in the Eucharist? Is the present-tense encounter with it an action in its own right? Is the metaphysical distinction between substance and accident germane to the action (that is, does it support it, neutralize it, or have no effect)? These are, of course, precise questions that deserve far greater attention than can be given here. However, let us here gesture toward answering the final question. It is important to be clear, though, that we are not merely pursuing a dogmatic non-sequitur but are attempting to combine several strands from Nietzsche within a Christian situation—one that is theological but also embodied, historical but also a present action, in the memory but not confined within the mind, tied to the past but also alive to it. Nietzsche would not have appreciated this particular line of inquiry but that is no reason to keep from pursuing it.

How then shall we attend to whether the metaphysical distinction between substance and accident is germane to the eucharistic action? If accidents were of no value at all, the celebration would cease to be a *meal* that nourishes the body as well as the soul. But bread and wine do, in fact, nourish the body. It is the case that bread symbolizes that which sustains life and wine symbolizes the joy of life.[23] Yet they do not *merely* symbolize these things; they actually enact them. A sensualist doctrine of the Eucharist rightly acknowledges the fact that the Eucharist involves the senses even while it misconstrues the nature of that involvement by attempting to include the body in a nourishment that can only properly make sense as being meant for the soul.[24] It has the appearance of attempting to bring together body and soul when, in fact, it continues to hold them apart. In other words, a sensualist Eucharist condescends to the senses of taste and touch even while it ceases to be food for the very body that possesses these senses; it therefore undervalues the senses.[25] In this way, even though transubstantiation relies on a metaphysical separation of substance and accident, one effect of its doing so is the uniting of two forms of nourishment within the body such that the soul has no hope of being fed on its own; it cannot even imagine it as Descartes presumably could.[26]

Nietzsche's own experience sought to understand the spiritual as an aspect of the body. In his madcap autobiography, *Ecce Homo*, he recounts that, "my muscular agility has always been greatest when my creative power has flowed most abundantly. The *body* is inspired: let us leave the 'soul' out of it."[27] More to the point, perhaps, his polemic against the dead mummies proudly on display in the comfortable chambers of his contemporaries underwrites his conviction that the study of history must serve life, meaning that *study* and *life* cannot name two separate things. Remembering the past must be an action with an adventure quotient insufficiently contained within the comfortable settings academics generally make for their minds (and with the support of their universities). If the practice of the Eucharist, therefore, strikes us as removed from the practice of theology, particularly from New Testament studies—a category mistake, if you will—then we are experiencing the tension Nietzsche sought to identify. It is one thing to investigate the life of the so-called historical Jesus, but we are well within a Nietzschian mode of critique if we insist that any scholar whose investigation does not also include participation in the active eucharistic life of the church is not only unfaithful to Christianity but is also a cowardly scholar. Whatever else may be said about the distinction between the historical Jesus and the Christ of faith, it is surely a distinction symptomatic of the inactive life of academics.

We should, of course, acknowledge that most human acts are not of this sort. That is, they do not display sacramental logic. The collective aspirations and efforts of a society may recall the glories of the past and press toward a better future. But the way it remembers will always be less than true to the way that its past has shaped its present social form. Either it will remember selectively or it will fail to remember at all. On the former, a society will call to mind only some things and not others, smoothing over the exigencies and vagaries of the past, aware that its identity is uncertain since that identity owes exclusively to the connections that will be made with the past. A society will not usually be tempted to block out the past, but instead to employ memory that is only conditioned by the will to maintain the successes of the present or to achieve new future ones. This is evident in how nations remember their wars—not only those it won, but those it lost. The way the United States of America recalls the painful memories of defeat in Vietnam, for example, as part of its larger, ongoing narrative of the triumph of "freedom" and "justice" in the world indicates how difficult it is for a people to remember the past truthfully while simultaneously accepting the political and social identity that that memory necessarily entails.[28]

In this respect, it seems that all societies are doomed to deceive themselves in attempts to evade the alternative: how to live with the thought that we are what we have done. Not only do we not want to own our terrible pasts—indeed, our pasts may often be more boring than terrible—but we also do not want to believe that our pasts limit our freedom. Hegel had split open the old binaries of God-world and man-nature by inserting the intentionally malleable third category: society-history. The new gaps this exposed are held open as the sites of human liberation, free from entrapment in one or the other side of the binary. The lonely individual standing unconditioned before God, and thus uniformly condemned, is freed toward the multifarious formation of his culture. For Hegel, one's past does not limit one's freedom but precisely generates it, yields up the plans for an infinitely variable escape from determinism. Historical knowledge, like all knowledge, is only partial, and historical knowledge of the present can never submit to a fully constructed system as a known quantity. Even so, this is precisely what Nietzsche charges had become of Hegel's philosophy. History had become a well-defined entrapment, the movement of history was still one of progress, but was now an automated process with a predictably unfolding future generated through careful disassembly of historical facts. Nietzsche could see, though, that precisely when freedom is grasped, it ceases to be freedom.

It is worth reflecting on this connection between freedom and self-deception. A culture's greatest lies to itself are those that underwrite its desires to think of itself as unconditioned by the events and choices of the past, that is, to think of itself as free. But to tell this lie successfully, it must alter the way it tells the past. It cannot be like the cattle and forget everything, but must remember, tell, and enact the past untruthfully. In Nietzsche's own day, this was revealed by the instability of the German fascination with history. The faux Greek columns of official buildings and wood painted to look like marble attempted to claim the authority of the past but only betrayed the anxiety of German identity.[29] The present culture was so evacuated of a genuine debt to the past that that past needed to be constructed, only all too obviously shown to be a product of the present's proclivity for fakeness. Put differently, the German culture suffered from the incompatibility of both a desire for freedom and a desire for a profound identity. But so long as "freedom" names the ability to narrate one's existence apart from one's past, that is, to identify oneself in terms other than historical ones, identity will not be able to extend any deeper than the seemingly arbitrary deeds of the present.

Nietzsche saw that his society's unbounded drive to consume knowledge was correlative of its loss of myth, which is to say, its loss of narrative identity. Fake Greek columns were merely monuments to the prejudices of bourgeois disquiet, to us perhaps embarrassingly incoherent in its contradictory wishes both to have a past and to be free from it. In such a situation, knowledge is disconnected from anything useful because it lacks a mythic structure, left merely to exist as "brute facts." The knower hovers above the fray, fearful that the act of knowing might jeopardize his freedom. But the self-deception necessary to maintain this hovering ironically cannot help but also take a narrative form, suggesting that the belief in brute facts is itself a myth, but precisely one that disguises itself. Persisting in believing it is yet another form of self-deception. In this way, Nietzsche's critique of historicism is related to his critique of realism; both had become ways of escaping the limitations of the past.

Moreover, there is a nearly opposite phenomenon that concerns Nietzsche, though it displays precisely the same untruthful relation with the past. From our vantage point, Nietzsche was nothing but prescient in his claims about the death of God in European thought and culture even while he noted widespread unwillingness to accept the loss of Christian morality that must accompany it. Even now, it is still common to find those who want to reject Christian metaphysics and theology while retaining, for example, a Christian sense of justice.[30] Perhaps it has become even more common, especially as tacit assent to Christian theological claims has continued to diminish in the century since Nietzsche. Nevertheless, just as Nietzsche hoped to recover the power of myth (with Wagner, in early stages) to fill the void left by the death of God in culture, he also came to resort to more drastic means. In his unpublished notes, he speaks of "The *greatest* of struggles: for this a new weapon is needed. The hammer: to provoke a fearful decision, to confront Europe with the consequences: whether its will 'wills' destruction. Prevention of reduction to mediocrity. Rather destruction!"[31]

Nietzsche feared that the European inability to face the moral consequences of its own intellectual claims would lead to nihilism, the mediocre resignation to contradiction, and the enervated culture of apathy that it would produce. I shall have more to say about this prognosis in the next chapter, but here let us mark how this European comportment is evidence of a selective rendering of the past. Insofar as the cultural memory preserved its Christian past (and here we see that Nietzsche's polemic was not just leveled against those who wanted to be served by their "memory" of the *Greek* past), it found itself needing to do so in a way that permitted a new distance from the claims that that past made on the present. To be sure, Nietzsche aspired for Europe to be able to overcome the past, to advance beyond the good and evil of Christian morality, and he was overcome with impatience at the general foot-dragging in this regard, the refusal to make decisive breaks with the past when necessary—the near absence of his "free spirits."

Nietzsche did not have a univocal doctrine of history, whether its total rejection to be free from it or its total attachment to the life of the present. Either mode may be appropriate to a people who have learned, as he thought they should, to give primary place to the present orientation of a culture. Then making self-confident use of the past or else self-consciously transcending it are both enlisted in a larger project. What he could not tolerate was a lack of self-consciousness that owed to a lazy submission to our already powerful propensity to lie to ourselves when confronted with a choice where the truth may be at stake, but so is our comfort—and comfort usually wins. Even though the ensuing years have witnessed countless ways that Europe has transcended its Christian past, Nietzsche would have appreciated recent cases like debates over which historical references to make in the preamble to a European Union Constitution. References to Europe's Greek and Roman roots as well as its Enlightenment and scientific traditions were readily agreed upon while papal recommendations to advocate for recognition of the Christian (primarily Catholic) role in shaping European identity were discarded. Nietzsche would have appreciated how it is easier to forget the past than to remember it in a new, larger way. He would no doubt have concluded that Europe actually has no real identity and so must abuse the past.

The claim that historicism and realism both sought to escape the limitations of the past exposes a deep irony. This is because, in one of its forms, historicism is actually meant to accomplish the opposite of this—it is meant to draw our attention to the way that our present is a social and historical product. But this can be a hard pill to swallow and in fact the nineteenth-century debates over historicism were often waged with the hope of disclosing an accompanying way out, a promise of salvation from the determinations of society and history. Rather than try to surpass Hegel, many sought to bring him to their own side by enlisting the promise of historical progress.[32] Dominating historicism was only a version of the domination of history by circumscribing it by reason in efforts to make it into a system.

History loses its usefulness for the present precisely through this rational will to dominate it. Nietzsche thought Hegel himself had betrayed his own best insights, initially enraptured by the French Revolution but, as time went on, disillusioned by it as many others were. Hegel's view of history changed too. Originally, it was one in which history was equal with life insofar as the moment was full of adventure and hope, the making and inheriting of history commingling in the life of a revolutionary people.

But, coincident with his disillusionment, Hegel made clever use of reason to evade the contradiction he must have felt.[33] He built the very idea of contradiction into his account of history such that history's meaning is revealed through the constant process of contradiction where, for example, disappointment and pain after a revolution is only part of history's ascendancy. This enabled Hegel to be right (in his theory of history) even when he was wrong (in his actual historical excitement at the storming of the Bastille). But this is a sign of disaster to Nietzsche because it allows one to evade the exigencies of reenactment, commemorating the past without performing it in the present. As we have seen, the fact that Nietzsche's age saw Germany enchanted with ideas of history and progress only attests to the seduction of history as a vehicle for evasion comparable to art and religion.[34] An interest in the study of history actually converts into a refusal to employ it precisely to the extent that it is studied as brute facts. The ironic detachment of German culture to its own history (which was often only imagined anyway), according to Nietzsche, was both produced by and furthered this interest.

A final consideration remains: what about forgiveness, that esteemed convention in which the past is connected with the present through liberty rather than limitation? Nietzsche admired the noble spirits who lived in merry apathy against the insults and wounds of the past. Their positive ambition and active approach to life (what Nietzsche would later come to call their will to power) has no room for the recollection of past devastation, no time for the sadness that sets in when mulling over not only the terrible things of the past but also when considering that the very existence of a past marks a profound limitation on the present. Unlike the overly sensitive souls who are overwhelmed by a single injustice—whom Nietzsche likens to one who bleeds to death from a scratch[35]—the noble soul marches on, even forgetting the past for its insignificance and only then able to forgive. Nietzsche thought of himself as a brilliant psychologist, with uncommon insight into human nature. He no doubt knew that we want to forget the horrors of the past because they are not only the source of present suffering insofar as we remember them, but worse, they are almost always a source of guilt. Furthermore, we fear asking for and receiving forgiveness because we are afraid that we will be separated from our pasts which, though they are horrible, nevertheless tell us who we are. But not so with the noble spirit who rises above these all too human foibles. Such a one does not fear forgetting the past as a function of nobility; he even loves his enemy, having so diminished the influence of the enemy on his life. Anything less, for Nietzsche, is evident of an insufficiently strong will and an enfeebled approach to life. Miroslav Volf rightly avers that this kind of forgetting—noble, strong, active—ranks as Nietzsche's alternative to Christian forgiveness.[36]

Christians must forgive through appeals to justice to specify the thing being forgiven as unjust. Nietzsche would not countenance justice functioning in this way since it invariably must make appeals to transcendent notions, often inflected eschatologically as in the Last Judgment. Forgetting to forgive posits the forgiver as the creator of a future in which there is no judgment apart from the discrimination of the forgiver-creator displayed in her exercise of forgetfulness. Such forgetfulness is not deliberate but is only a function of her creative activity in which some things are simply closed off because of other things that are being opened up in being created. Despite his metaphysical objections, a Christian account of memory and forgiveness will still charge Nietzsche for having evaded the question of whether one may forgive something that is yet remembered. At the least, it would be perverse to remember the suffering of Christ without forgiveness, especially given the active (eucharistic) remembrance of *this particular past* that Nietzsche's critiques of a historical consciousness would seem to endorse.

Eucharistically, then, the memory of Christ's suffering is a memory of the *grounds* for forgiveness and the reconciliation of estranged parties—God and humanity, Jew and Gentile. Christian thought has always affirmed the work of Christ as accomplishing this, even where it has disputed how it does so. But the Eucharist does more than remember the grounds of forgiveness. As reenactment, Christian suffering participates in the suffering of Christ, in the willful obedience to God's righteousness which, in a sinful world, may certainly lead to death. The saints join the angels in remembering-through-singing the slain Lamb while affirming by their singing that the wrongful slaying of the Lamb has become the decisive juncture for establishing his worth to be worshipped.

The wrongs Christ suffered in the crucifixion are not obliterated for the sake of performing the forgiveness of the cross (which is an absurdity), but the cross is re-signified by the resurrection, the gift of glory to the Son, by which the world is granted the possibility itself to forgive wrongs insofar as it submits its present meaning and constitution to the re-narration and transformation that the resurrection is. Not only do Christians rehearse forgiving those who made Christ suffer, which some have suspected is really only a thinly cloaked form of retribution if not a horrific occasion for singling out Jews for blame. But more to the point, the forgiveness of humanity is made possible by that very suffering. Insofar as we forgive, therefore, we are able to tell the horrors of the past in the presence of those who have wronged us, something Nietzsche's noble forgetting can never allow. This suggests that the forgiveness he envisions is not actually forgiveness, but only oblivion.

Nietzsche's positive ethic, it must be admitted, places no particular value on forgiveness but only on the way of life that strives for creative use of all resources, especially including anything that might otherwise limit and constrain. His creators are future-oriented masters of their wills, themselves the antidote to the puerilities of modern culture. They are the subject of the following chapter.

Chapter 4
Un-meaning history

Seemingly only minutes before beginning work on what he was to consider his greatest creation, *Thus Spoke Zarathustra*, Nietzsche set out a prosaic précis of his prophet Zarathustra's central message: Eternal Recurrence of the same.[1]

> *The heaviest weight.* — What if some day or night a demon were to steal into your loneliest loneliness and say to you: "This life as you now live it and have lived it you will have to live once again and innumerable times again; and there will be nothing new in it, but every pain and every joy and every thought and sigh and everything unspeakably small or great in your life must return to you, and in the same succession and sequence—even this spider and this moonlight between the trees, and even this moment and I myself. The eternal hourglass of existence is turned over again and again, and you with it, speck of dust!" Would you not throw yourself down and gnash your teeth and curse the demon who spoke thus? Or have you once experienced a tremendous moment when you would have answered him: "You are a god, and never have I heard anything more divine." If this thought gained power over you, as you are it would transform and possibly crush you; the question in each and everything, "Do you want this again and innumerable times again?" would lie on your actions the heaviest weight! Or how well disposed would you have to become to your self and to life *to long for nothing more fervently* than for this ultimate eternal confirmation and seal?[2]

It is clear from this extraordinary passage that Nietzsche intends for Eternal Recurrence to function more as a moral category than an ontological one. It is a challenge and a dare to the *will* more than an assertion about the way things are, which is the reason he begins by asking "what if . . . ?" What kind of person is required to be able to respond, "*this* is divine?" How much strength—what kind of strength—is necessary to greet the return of one's life, even in its moments of execrable grief, with delight? Do such people even now exist? These are questions about the moral will. As time went on, it is true, Nietzsche became more fascinated with the idea of Eternal Recurrence as an ontological concept. But he never would have come to that point had he not been so captivated by the moral will vital for its acceptance in the first place, quite regardless of its status as *fact*. The person of strength, the *Übermensch*, summons the will to endure the seemingly tragic possibility that nothing in the universe can be improved. This is not a will commensurate with nihilism but precisely the reverse: only the will that displays the strength to continue celebrating life as Eternal Recurrence can resist nihilism. Nietzsche attributed the real tragedy to that situation in which metaphysical claims continue to hold forth promise to those souls unable either to accept the state of the world as it is or to acknowledge that life is nevertheless worth living. The death of God makes room for the Eternal Recurrence. This means that displacing the reach of the metaphysical thesis owes less to convictions we call ontological and more to those we call moral (that is, *will* displaces *being*): the ability to say "this is divine" supersedes the reality of this new, *immanent* divinity.

As some of his unpublished notes suggest, Nietzsche was profoundly overtaken by the weight of this new doctrine and planned to write a book by the title *The Eternal Recurrence: A Prophecy*, except that he wanted to wait until he had scientific proof to support it.[3] He even considered taking up a course of study in the natural sciences to pursue such proof. At the same time, though, he knew that the impact of the doctrine in all of its deep resonances could not be reduced to the level of scientific proof. His abortive attempt to prove the doctrine is uncharacteristic of the main thrust of his thought, especially given his genealogical refutation of the doctrine's obverse, namely God's existence. As was observed in Chapter 2, the provability of the latter is actually counter-productive with respect to its truth; a provable God cannot be true. But Nietzsche's brief sojourn with the idea that science may hold the key to Eternal Recurrence (we may envisage the grand cosmological claims of astrophysics about space and time, for example) surely betrays his diffidence toward more resolutely taking leave of the canons of naturalism and materialism that held sway in his day.[4] After all, the reason he himself believed it was not because it was proved to him or that he was convinced by a rigorous dialectical argument about the nature of existence; but he felt himself rising to the challenge to believe it, what he called "the highest formula of affirmation that can possibly be attained."[5] A will that awaits proof of Eternal Recurrence will always be insufficient for accepting it. Those who can accept it take joy in uncertainty rather than certainty, contingency rather than necessity, and consequently elevate themselves over those whom it drives to despair. This stark social division between the weak and the strong that Nietzsche imagined corresponded to the strength of will he thought necessary for the affirmation of life in the face of history's ruthless, nihilistic drift. It was more essential, then, that the doctrine is *important* than that it is *true*. What is this doctrine?

Eternal Recurrence is Nietzsche's answer to the question about history's meaning. In brief, it goes like this. In the late nineteenth century, science was explicating concepts like the law of conservation of energy, the idea that the amount of energy in the universe remains constant even while its various forms (heat, light, exchanges with matter) are constantly changing. Apparently inspired by this ("The law of the conservation of energy demands *eternal recurrence*."[6]), Nietzsche thought through a radical cosmology that falls along parallel lines. Its logic is that time is infinite and within this time, every possible combination of things and events must surely occur at least once; the span of infinite time will exhibit every permutation of distinct entities within innumerable episodes, and not only of those entities that now exist and are known to us but precisely also those things hidden from us as having possible existence yet hidden only by time rather than nature's "laws." Time is dynamic and literally full of possibilities. But Nietzsche reasoned that he must go further than this. If all things occur in infinite time, and if time is truly infinite, every occurrence must not only occur once but must occur an infinite number of times. If, from the present moment (and so every moment), eternity stretches backward to infinity then every moment has already happened in precisely the same way; the distance from "now" to the future and the past never changes, and not because things are static; they are dynamic in their *infinity*. Even the idea of the Eternal Recurrence must eternally recur.[7]

Only those with the requisite courage could accept this. In some ways too, only the courageous can understand how weighty it is. Nietzsche's Zarathustra concludes that, among all of the animals, humans are the most courageous and so potentially can see into the depths of life, unafraid of seeing all of life's suffering. The greater the courage, the more suffering is seen even while the most courageous will *still* be able to proclaim in the face of that suffering, "Was *that* life? Well then! Once more!"[8] The courage necessary to accept Eternal Recurrence is identical with the courage necessary to continue living with the sufferings of history without being overcome by resentment. As we will discuss in Chapter 5, Nietzsche took Christian morality to be the outcome of this kind of resentment—an inability otherwise to reconcile wrongs suffered with the lack of power to do anything about it, an inability that finally yields concepts like eternal judgment and the exaltation of the humble and meek. For now, though, we can notice how it is possible to resent Eternal Recurrence itself, its lack of resolution for wrongs suffered, its complete absence of future vindication. This was an intentional tactic for Nietzsche and no doubt a reason he tended to speak about it in hushed tones to his friends just as Zarathustra's voice becomes increasingly soft as he speaks about it.[9] In short, only the *Übermensch* can accept the doctrine of Eternal Recurrence and, because the way one accepts the doctrine is by also accepting the coming of the *Übermensch*, this means that only the *Übermensch* can accept the doctrine of the *Übermensch*!

Why does this matter? It matters precisely because we see here an example of the kind of knowledge Nietzsche thought really mattered. As we have discussed in earlier chapters, knowledge is more than information since no facts precede meaning, the saliency of which is preeminently illustrated by Nietzsche's sometimes aphoristic style. Likewise, knowledge of the *Übermensch* and Eternal Recurrence can only be heard as true by those with the will to accept it as true. In other words, their comprehension of these things is not separable from their assent to them. On the one hand, even though Zarathustra only heralds the coming of the *Übermensch* and never claims to be the latter, he must on the other hand actually be the *Übermensch* himself at least insofar as the herald of this doctrine must have the will to accept it as true. Still, perhaps he is more properly thought of as a John the Baptist character who prepares the way; the *Übermensch* seemingly would not be bothered with teaching others (since a herald of such news must be redundant insofar as nothing he can say will have a force of explanation beyond what is needed for belief by the assenting will).

However, let us register an objection against this style of reasoning, particularly if it feels like a trap, forcing the hand of those it would try to convince. Are those with wills insufficient to accept the Eternal Recurrence really unworthy to understand it and vice versa? Can it not be the case that some will reject it, not because they have misunderstood it, but because they have understood it only too well? Is Nietzsche really commending fideism in such a facile manner? The answer must finally be "No," not only because these questions, while at home in analytic discourse are foreign to Nietzsche's thinking but also because the acceptance of Eternal Recurrence involves more than assenting to a seemingly impossible proposition; it also names its practical incorporation into one's life. Near the very end of Nietzsche's lucid life, he was still rejoicing in his discovery that the affirmation of existence entails a desire for its eternal return, an inspiration he first received seven years earlier. Positing that the disjunction between truth and falsehood is seated in the will, he writes in *Ecce Homo* in 1888,

> How much truth can a spirit *bear*, how much truth can a spirit *dare*? That became for me more and more the real measure of value. . . . error is cowardice . . . Every acquisition, every step forward in knowledge is the *result* of courage, of severity towards oneself, of cleanliness with respect to oneself.[10]

The courage to believe the truth, then, is more fundamental than truth. To affirm the Dionysian character of the Eternal Recurrence is to uphold the existence of the world as it is apart from any underlying meaning or selective rendering of only life's presentable side: *amor fati*, the love of fate, Nietzsche says, is his new love.[11] This is a deeply agonizing and ecstatic prospect, requiring the subjugation of self-fascination and vanity to the cold logic of a universe that is unremittingly on the march through an equally arctic temporal infinity. The *Übermensch* is found where this chill is also *simultaneously* a balmy muse.

A clarification Nietzsche made to the doctrine is in how it attests to the constant state of flux in which the universe subsists. Because we do not observe that the forces of the world have reached equilibrium, they must *never* reach equilibrium.[12] If time extends infinitely in both directions—past and future—then the discordant forces that stir alongside and against each other have by now already thrown up every conceivable recipe; but the discordance still persists. This tells us something about the nature of the forces at work, namely, that they are *inherently* at odds with each other, if they could be harmonized, they would have done so by now. We have already encountered the importance of this aspect of nature for Nietzsche and here it serves another function. It might seem as though the Eternal Recurrence positively contradicts flux and requires stasis since if all events eternally recur *ad infinitum*, it can sound like the ultimate predictability, as far removed from constant change as possible. If everything returns, do we not know the future in knowing the present while being powerless to do anything about it? But Nietzsche does not rule out change in advance (which would make his doctrine take on the worst aspects of theory). Instead, he begins with the empirical, the observation that there is change and concludes that change must therefore be constitutive of the nature of things.

Ethically, the Eternal Recurrence converts crudely into a kind of categorical imperative: Live every moment as though you will be living it over and over again for eternity. Unlike Kant's rule, the ethical import of the Eternal Recurrence is not primarily on the rightness or wrongness of individual actions. It is not "always act in such a way that you can will that this is what you will be doing countless times," as though one determines the nature of eternity through one's agency. Instead, the most salutary actions will be those that are, in fact, playful even in the midst of life's greatest trials. This is the true affirmation of life. Fate sets the stage on which life is lived and so no human actions have intrinsic value simply as actions, but only inasmuch as they are still able to take to the stage, uncontrollable as it is; this puts Nietzsche at odds with Kant's scheme. Likewise, the great separation between what we can control and what we cannot is immaterial to this ethic, placing it at odds with utilitarianism that posits the goodness of acts based on their ability to control things. Nietzsche was proud to have discovered an ethical injunction that did not make appeals to another standard, to otherworldly ideals. Instead, it is the world as it is that functions as its own norm. This doctrine pronounced by his prophet Zarathustra was a way of remaining true to the earth. There is no metaphysical disjunction between this world and eternity since what is here and now is already a participation in the eternal. There is no heaven and hell where rewards and punishments are meted out, no distant promise of the alleviation of suffering.

There is also no creation because, like Aristotle over against his medieval Christian, Jewish, and Muslim interpreters, Nietzsche holds that the universe has always existed. Nietzsche is not primarily against creation on scientific grounds, but as with so many things, on moral grounds. He objects to the desire to explain things on account of creation, in which he always detects a hidden theological motive.

> *The new world-conception.*— The world exists; is it not
> something that becomes, not something that passes away.
> Or rather: it becomes, it passes away, but it has never begun
> to become and never ceased from passing away—it main-
> tains itself in both. . . . We need not worry for a moment
> about the hypothesis of a *created* world. The concept
> "create" is today completely indefinable, unrealizable;
> merely a word, a rudimentary survival from the ages of
> superstition; one can explain nothing with a mere word [13]

Nietzsche might have been content if creation was thought of as just a fact, like the existence of the earth. But like the other great watchdogs of ideology of that era, he could not bear the drive to explain things (too easily, one is tempted to say) that issues from moral cowardice, a failure to accept the present reality of the world as it is. Without creation and without a *goal*, such reality can never be passed off as becoming something better, returning to its intended, original state, or otherwise pregnant with meaning known to those whose knowledge of the present world therefore is *better* for knowing where it all came from and is going. This is an ethic that promises no salvation and posits no rescue. It strives to be purely immanentist. Whether it is true or not is somewhat beside the point insofar as the one who is able to handle it, to incorporate it into living, is the one who can overcome the haunting reality of a world spinning alone in the universe. Such a one is Nietzsche's *Übermensch*.

The one who accepts the Eternal Recurrence can *affirm* everything for what it is rather than for what it is promised to become. Nietzsche provided a link with the eternal that did not diminish the temporal exactly inasmuch as what is temporal *is* what is eternal, through recurrence rather than correspondence (worldly things correspond to heavenly things), ends (worldly things await an eternal determination), or any other means whereby temporal and eternal are kept separated. "I seek an eternity for everything."[14] Thus, Nietzsche's rejection of meaning is not a way of disclaiming reality; his claim is that if one requires meaning to affirm things, one can never truly affirm things as they are since any affirmation will always be tied to a condition extrinsic to the thing being affirmed. He does not exactly claim there is no such thing as meaning, as we might suppose, but that there is nothing besides the earth in which we can find meaning and the *Übermensch* is the meaning of the earth. As the *amor fati* dictates, "one should not wish things to be otherwise, not before and not after, in the whole of eternity."[15]

This bears some elaboration because it potentially sounds so counter-intuitive, if not completely mistaken.[16] We usually assume that someone who does not want anything changed has resigned himself to a powerless existence, has given up on doing anything productive, of making the world a better place. Yet Nietzsche's ethic decidedly purports not to be an ethic of resignation, a quality he instead pins on the culture of the "last man," as will be shown below. One way to make sense of this is to acknowledge that affirmation of existence is not itself an ethic for Nietzsche but is both a disposition and the outcome of the one who lives the ethic. It is only by affirming the integrity of earthly existence as the only kind there is that the *Übermensch* is enabled to devote himself to creating a new future for the earth. But if the integrity of existence, earthly or otherwise, entails being bound by the reality of Eternal Recurrence, "determined" by the laws of nature as we find them, powerless to overcome them, how free can his "free spirits" really be? How can they be creators in any sense at all?

The overcoming creativity that characterizes Nietzsche's ethics needs to take seriously that the Eternal Recurrence is a kind of naturalistic determinism even while it will not allow determinism to devolve into fatalism. This is the precise tension that requires an overcoming will—*not* the overcoming of Eternal Recurrence, which is a motivation he finds among philosophers and theologians alike, but overcoming the paralyzing effect it might otherwise have. We can appreciate how difficult it is to conceive of these things non-fatalistically. After all, the one who does so may have a *happiness* of sorts, but we are perhaps disinclined to share in that happiness because it is so evident that things in life are not always as they should be. But it is precisely this "should be" that Nietzsche wants to eradicate because it implies a goal that he takes to be indefensible, morally and otherwise. He is not resigned to the events of history as though their existence means something, as though the *fact* that something happens means that it was *meant* to happen, that these events rather than others are the ones that should be.

"Should be" is the language of *telos*, of ends, and Nietzsche argues against it in both of its senses. One form of *telos* is a consideration of an action's consequences and in this regard, as was shown above, Nietzsche is opposing the utilitarianism of his English contemporary, John Stewart Mill. For Mill, certain actions should be performed and others not performed based on how they generate benefit and maximize happiness and pleasure. But Nietzsche thinks that this is not true to how we act: "Man does *not* strive for pleasure; only the Englishman does."[17] And, in a fantastically entertaining even if ultimately pretentious set of remarks, Nietzsche accuses the "English moralists" (Mill and Bentham, especially) of mistaking bourgeois English prejudices for a universal code of morality.[18] They are hiding their peculiarly English vices under a veneer of scientific reasoning and calculation.

What is wrong with this is both the self-deception involved and the unrealistic one-size-fits-all approach to morality: "the demand for one morality for all is detrimental to precisely the higher men."[19] The "higher men," of course, have no need for a morality that calculates things, that measures one good against another, which determines aggregates of benefit and the maximization of benefit and happiness. Their actions have merit for their own sakes, not for what they aim to accomplish. They do not stop to consider outcomes but boldly take risks. The *Übermensch* will therefore be happy and we will know him by his happiness, even though he does not become the *Übermensch* by pursuing happiness. Happiness is not instrumental toward anything else (as Aristotle noted) and neither is it sought directly. It is only "achieved" indirectly, by pursuing other things for their own sakes. This is an ancient ethic that, for Nietzsche, merely worked to expose the mistaken priorities of his contemporaries for whom happiness could itself constitute an analytic code of morality.

Another sense of *telos* is that of the final good, as found in Aristotle's metaphysics and ethics. According to this sense, we know what something is because of its *telos*, what it is *for*. This idea is shot through with notions of design and quasi-divine purpose that Nietzsche rejects. For him, the meaning of things is not found in what things are for but in how we use them; our use of them *becomes* what things are for. What Nietzsche is most opposed to is the givenness of meaning and purpose, those things that are revealed about the world that we would not otherwise know. Aristotle, it must be said, also understood purpose to reside in the use of things even though his appropriators subsequently found God in the final good of things, the meaning for which things exist—their destiny. What then is meant by the use of a thing? Nietzsche does not oppose our acting toward things purposively or using things meaningfully; he only specifies that the meaning and purpose do not precede our use, presaging Wittgenstein's later philosophy that applies "meaning in use" to language. We use a thing by custom and so things do our bidding, which is to say that *we* make the final good of everything we use. Yet Nietzsche diagnosed our timidity at this specific point, our reluctance to find new uses for old things.

Nietzsche even seemed to acknowledge that he was fated to be misunderstood and rejected on those topics he considered most important. By the time his writings were appreciated beyond a very small audience mostly made up of friends, he was in no frame of mind to know it. One of his early books, *Human, All Too Human*, only circulated in review and complimentary copies while the rest of the copies sat in a warehouse. It is as astonishing that Nietzsche continued to write and publish, as it is understandable that he felt more and more that his words were falling on deaf ears. Should his admonitions against resentment and toward a positive, though often unrewarding, life of strength be read self-referentially? When Zarathustra realizes that "I am not the mouth for these ears," he decides to appeal to the people's pride by describing for them the "last man."[20] We need not be surprised, I think, to find that Nietzsche's description here is richly colored.

The last man is content with extremely small pleasures—or as we may surmise: *too small to be pleasurable*? Pleasures are only comforts; and those things that otherwise would give the most intense pleasure (like friendship) almost cease to exist, often persisting in name only. Love of neighbor is reduced to serving a mere utilitarian function, namely, the rubbing of bodies together for the sake of warmth. This last crude, physical image of the Hobbsian social contract recalls the way that human social relations may fail to aspire to anything beyond the few items needed for survival when divested of a notion of human flourishing. But it is not the individual "last man" that matters; he is not a hero nor is he self-made. Nietzsche's last man is generated and produced by an entire culture of resignation for whom great things are always in the past and are only ever approximated through selective memories.

Such a man denotes not only the ebb of human achievement but also the judicious balance of those resources that make themselves all too plain to the cultural observer, those things that are at the obvious disposal of everyone exactly because everyone takes them for granted. No one seeks what is new but only repackages artifacts from the past. The culture of the last man will never become great because its horizon for "greatness" is radically foreshortened. It is satisfied with a small degree of pleasure and happiness, believing that such things are sufficient for life itself, and so does not expect very much from its cultural products, social works, or heroic individuals, if it has any at all. It is easier to obey than to rule, easier to sanction the status quo than to quarrel with the limits of what is possible based on what has happened so far. "One virtue is more than two" for the *Übermensch*, "because it is more of a noose on which his catastrophe may hang."[21] The life of virtue is seldom simply rewarded or straightforwardly a mixture of qualities that underwrite a balanced life, a life without quarrel in which opposing sides are synthesized within the virtuous person. Even the last man, the "greatest danger for all of man's future," is called good and just.[22] However, the singular passion of individual virtue dramatically raises the stakes and imperils the one who would cling to it at all costs.

It is evident that Nietzsche's hatred for the last man is tied to his hatred of theology. In his understanding, or at least the understanding he pins on the last man, the very nature of what it means for something to be "last" depends on a doctrine of creation in exact opposition to which last things—the things of which eschatology speaks—are established. "Last" then means "end," a construction that is only possible if there was a beginning. The last man is discharged by theology and as a construct derides the kind of satisfaction that will accompany a people who rely on significances outside of themselves so long as they consider themselves creations rather than creators. In rejecting creation in favor of Eternal Recurrence, Nietzsche was necessarily rejecting eschatology in favor of the *Übermensch*. The last man relies on a seemingly inevitable process, powerless to control the future which is destined to complete the cycle set in motion by creation—for his life, this "determinism" is fatal. It is mistaken to read Nietzsche as adducing that the death of God must now mean that life is reduced to the bald pursuit of pleasure. It is instead the last man (and not Nietzsche himself) who, like Augustine's godless pagan, pursues pleasure on the assumption that meaning is a given reality exhaustively circumscribed by known values.

The venerable Thomist philosopher, Josef Pieper, thinks that there is a "grain of truth in nihilism." He has in mind the way that Christianity can and generally does affirm a kind of *annihilatio* that militates against too exalted a doctrine of human creativity and agency. Pieper follows Aquinas in affirming that if God alone creates, brings all that exists out of nothingness into existence, then God is capable of bringing creatures back to nothingness.[23] This would not be evil of God to do, Aquinas reasons, because the state of non-existence "before" creation was not an evil state. Even though existence is good, non-existence is simply neutral. Furthermore, on account of creation's disordered state that owes to sin, annihilation of all that exists may actually be countenanced as a positive act of justice on God's part. Thus if creation is not simply a past event but an ongoing act that persists uninterrupted, nothingness is the cessation of creation rather than a part of it (such as would be its conclusion and fulfillment). If this is the grain of truth in nihilism, it also invites clarification of the ways that Nietzsche's charge against the theological last man fails to ring true of Christian theology.

As just intimated, creation *ex nihilio* is that theological tradition that posits an understanding of creation that is not an event relegated to the past. Against many other philosophies, creation *ex nihilio* rejects God as an organizing principle of matter that preexisted the universe in eternal past time; God is truly a creator, creating the formlessness of the earth, as the first chapter of Genesis states, not from earlier, even more formless matter, but from literally nothing. Even time itself is part of the creation God makes so that we say that creation did not take place in time but is itself the very condition of possibility for timefulness. This is partly the reason that Christian thought, in following this tradition, confesses the timefulness of creation—not as an event in the past, however, but as the full character of existence. Creation is the continual presence of God to creation, upholding it at every point in love. Put differently, God did not create in six days and then stop creating. As Abraham Heschel asks, what did God create on the seventh day? The answer is that he created the Sabbath. God did so precisely by *making* something for what he had created—rest—and *inhabiting* it himself.[24] God's rest is crucially an action rather than the cessation of action; the Sabbath is not the absence of creative power, but God's positive presence to his creation.[25] Annihilation can therefore not be a positive act of destruction but must be the withdrawal of God's creativity from its object (another reason why if God were to annihilate, it could not be called an evil—it is not an act at all). God resting on the Sabbath did not eliminate creation for this reason. This Christian theological account is meant to safeguard a distinction between God and creatures which Aquinas took to be fundamental: existence is part of God's nature, part of what it is for God to be God; the existence of creatures is an entirely contingent aspect of a creature's nature. So, while creatures can cease to exist without contradiction, it is God's essence to exist.[26]

Therefore, despite his anti-theological position, Nietzsche was actually right infamously to reckon, not so much with a God who does not exist, but with a dead God. His atheism is appropriately phrased in this respect. Lesser foes than Nietzsche treat the question of God's existence in a misleading way when they say nothing else about God's nature. Christians profess a living God, that is, one who acts in the world. Therefore, as we have already observed, rather than oppose the traditional arguments for God's existence, Nietzsche gives an account of how and why the belief in God arose in the first place. Whatever may be said about the accuracy of this genealogy is beside the point when we are considering how this methodology corresponds to the Christian theological claim that a God who is not a living God (that is, a dead God) is not God at all. Nietzsche's gospel *must* be that "we have killed him" if he maintains the ascendancy of his new creators: *we* created God and so only *we* can kill him; *that* is why he does not exist.

On this account, then, killing God is an act of creation, a kind of eschatological move that opposes the original creation of God. It is not the passive nihilism of the last man, nor is it annihilation in the Christian sense since the mode of new creation the *Übermensch* enacts is not intrinsic to the original creation; killing God is a positive act. The new creation of moral values and the destruction of the old ones coincide in the actions of the *Übermensch*: "The annihilator of morals, the good and the just [mainstays of the old morality] call me."[27] It needs to be this way for Nietzsche because of the opposite story he tells about how the creation of God includes the creation of the end of all things insofar as the fate of things is subsequently transferred into God's hands. Humanity's creation of God, therefore, included within its own creative action the willing forgetfulness that we are creators. This is why, unlike the *Übermensch*, the last man would rather *consume* than create. The act of creation is left to others along with the energies that make one a creator (since the last man still believes God is the creator). Consumption is for those who seek comfort in those things mass-produced and with mass-appeal, the latter functioning as a precise gauge of the extent of a society's disillusionment with its own ability to do anything new. It is a society obsessed with security, with a will only to protect a leisure-lifestyle, though it may simultaneously lack the capacity to articulate its preference for leisure over creativity on account that it will likely be deceived into thinking that its consuming is its creating. Zarathustra underestimates the proclivity for self-deception and so chooses to play to the people's pride and vanity, distinguishing for them the life of creativity from the life of indifference.

Nevertheless, in a cruel reversal of fortunes and certainly contrary to his intentions, Zarathustra's description actually appeals to the people. "Turn us into these last men!" they shout. They ask for the last man to become him. They do not want to rise above the herd, but find comfort in their herd-identity, collectively wishing to become even more the epitome of the disengaged, passive, lackluster character described for them. For Nietzsche, this must only demonstrate how theological the people are, how much they wish for creation to be fulfilled by a reduction to nothingness. They yearn for nihilism though they do not know it. Perhaps even that which exists as last possesses the allure of accomplishment, even if it is a wholly passive one that relies on submissive agents to an overriding course of events—but to be included in it, even to be given a special place in it intimates the pitiable condition of the last man.

Zarathustra appeals to the people's pride. Yet he discovers not that the people's pride is too great, but that it is not great enough. Their pride was calibrated according to the culture of the herd in its present state. While Zarathustra imagines that even this people will pride themselves in their education, that is, their capacity to cause some to rise above others, in fact their sights do not extend beyond the education necessary to produce the last man (as opposed to the *Übermensch*, as Zarathustra obviously hopes).

He laments that "one day this soil will be poor and domesticated, and no tall tree will be able to grow in it."[28] Saddened by the people's reaction to his words, their impoverished pride, and his own miscalculations, Zarathustra seeks followers in other places, far from the crowded but ultimately barren marketplace. Having discovered that the emergence of the last man quite possibly may actually be the last thing, not only despite the words of the prophet Zarathustra but even ironically hastened by them, he leaves the marketplace to its own fate and turns to find a sympathetic hearing elsewhere. "Never again shall I speak to the people: for the last time have I spoken to the dead." He will seek out "whoever still has ears for the unheard-of."[29]

A people must produce the last man to make way for the *Übermensch* to emerge; they must court the dangerous possibility of nihilism and peer into the abyss before they can appreciate the need to summon the will not to fall headlong into it. The people's own dissatisfaction with their production of the last man will become the impetus for their will to produce the *Übermensch*, that is, the one who risks unbounded creativity, having seen how high the stakes really are: create or be annihilated. Even so—and because of this—Zarathustra will not set out a program for this production since it is precisely the *will* of the people that is in question. No words outlining a positive program can substitute for stirring the people's will to discover the steps that they will need to take to surpass what they have accomplished thus far. No doubt, Zarathustra knows that the will to produce the *Übermensch* will issue first in the courage to experiment and to test by taking risks, improvising on a new theme that operates on the far edges of the people's competency. This is because their will so to produce will always exceed their competency, becoming the soil of further virtue, even virtue not yet seen as such.[30]

The collective will to produce the *Übermensch* will also be the cause that will unite the people. Here we see Nietzsche's refusal to isolate *will* as a primary good on its own, that is to say, apart from a qualifier. By *itself*, will is nothing since there are a multitude of wills expressed for trivial ends. On this point, Nietzsche found that he needed to exceed and qualify Schopenhauer since it is by no means obvious that an unqualified will could be successfully invoked at any level to identify the basic orientation of the self and society. He asks, "Is 'will to power' a *kind* of 'will' or identical with the concept 'will'?" To which he answers that

> this will *does not exist at all*, that instead of grasping the idea of the development of one definite will into many forms, one has eliminated the character of the will by subtracting from its content, its "whither?"—this is in the highest degree the case with Schopenhauer: what he calls "will" is a mere empty word.[31]

This critique of Schopenhauer points to Nietzsche's own confidence that the actual activity of the will—its actual willing—is more basic than the idea of will, especially since *as an idea* it proves too difficult to pin down with any assurance. More precisely, and in a way that became increasingly important to Nietzsche, the will to power always functions as an activity that is only realized in action rather than being realized in the satisfaction of what it desires. Hunger is a will to eating and is satisfied when one eats. But the will to power differs from this by being satisfied in the *struggle* against those things that stand in its way, those things that directly oppose it.[32] This can be confusing because in making struggle a necessary component to the will to power, opposition and resistance are likewise made necessary. But then we might ask whether the will to overcome opposition is a true desire or not. If the will to power simultaneously wills overcoming and also wills the obstacles it must overcome, is it not thrust into a paradox? If we consider the desires of the will to power in the same way that we think about hunger (simultaneously willing the presence and absence of food), it is indeed a paradox. But the will to power will always seek out new and different challenges to overcome, restless for more when the object of struggle has been obtained or overcome: "with *possession* desire for possession always ceases."[33] This is not the same as saying that such desire never wants to be satisfied, that the will never wants to overcome, as though just-having-overcome is a state so undesirable that it foregoes the will to overcome. What the will to power desires, therefore, is not a state at all; satisfaction is found in its exercise rather than the outcome of its exercise.

As it turns out, then, we may surmise that hunger is not actually very different from the will to power after all. The pleasures of eating are not unrelated to the opposition eating encounters in the feeling of hunger; food would bring no pleasure if one were never hungry. The deferral of pleasure or satisfaction is really internal to the pleasure that the will seeks since it is precisely in the activity of seeking and opposing resistance that the will is most engaged. After all, Zarathustra counsels, "You should love peace as a means to new wars—and the short peace more than the long. To you I do not recommend work but struggle. To you I do not recommend peace but victory."[34] Struggle denotes a life of constantly changing engagement. It is never the staid and single-minded pursuit of inert goals, perceived for their goodness ahead of encountering them, promising to acquaint the seeker with treasures as known quantities. Such goals can only be dissatisfying to a life of motion since a life lived in possession of them requires no movement just as a life lived in pursuit of them is no life at all, only a long dying process, a winding down of life's energies in approach of death. Life simply *is* will to power, for Nietzsche, since its reverse, the will to any settled state, is life's slow dispossession.

Why must Zarathustra labor to secure an audience? As before, we might ask whether the problem is that Zarathustra's message is difficult to *understand* or difficult to *accept*. To be sure, the people misunderstand both that the last man is not worthy of admiration and also as a result, that they are themselves the last man insofar as they miss this point. In this sense, their souls are too corrupt to acknowledge that their misunderstanding is a moral failure— precisely a failure of *will*—rather than a function of simple ignorance that might be overcome through education. For Zarathustra, "education" typifies the way that a society thinks of itself as Enlightened when, in reality, its higher degrees only sanction and congratulate the ascendancy of the society in the current moment.[35] The kind of ignorance he encounters is not of the kind that is overcome in the usual ways. Zarathustra needs *willing* souls, not just those who have more knowledge. His message, therefore, like the Eternal Recurrence itself, is difficult to understand exactly to the extent that it is difficult to accept. The two operate on the same register since the will to accept it *is itself* the act of understanding it. In this respect, Zarathustra is just like all prophets who encounter the ignorance of stubborn wills and craven desires ("unrighteous!" cry the Hebrew prophets—this is their misunderstanding) and not uneducated hordes; Isaiah tells of a people who go into exile due to their lack of knowledge, precisely their dissolute wills.[36]

Nietzsche too would only know himself as a failed prophet. Not only did his writings largely fall on deaf ears during his lifetime but also, since then, he has often been misunderstood in ways that parallel the ways the people in the marketplace misunderstood Zarathustra. The people heard a message of nihilism, but they embraced rather than shunned it. They stood at the edge of the abyss but felt nothing but numbness. For Nietzsche, nihilism is a warning, a prescient glance down the road into a future where humanity refuses to cope with the death of God. He was not *advocating* nihilism, but declaring the way that it can and must be avoided. That said, clarifying Nietzsche's position in this regard is not aided by comments Nietzsche himself made in which he claims to be a nihilist: "the first perfect nihilist of Europe" and his description of the denial of the "true world," a position his philosophy enjoins, as nihilism, even as *a divine way of thinking*.[37] There is a certain amount of scholarly interest in whether such comments as these should be taken programmatically and normatively, especially given that all such references are from Nietzsche's unpublished notes and often display a kind of playful reversal of perspective in which he seems to be adopting the nomenclature of nihilism which his thought cannot help but resemble when looked at by those who are themselves most entrenched in its throes.[38]

This makes Nietzsche's *Thus Spoke Zarathustra* a book "for all and none," as its subtitle decrees. The message it proclaims is intended for everyone, yet only a few will be able to embrace it. Those who do not embrace it are doomed to misunderstand it or at least recast its central themes in ways that allow them to evade its application to their world. When Nietzsche refers to himself as a nihilist, he is making ironic use of that language in a way that panders to the ways that his detractors—Christians, Platonists—must regard his philosophy.[39] In reality, for him, it is the way of life of the strong, those who withstand the desire to locate the meaning of life's values in the objective sense afforded by a metaphysics on its way out, that allows one to overcome nihilism. Nihilism names the belief that existence is meaningless; to those who hold out not only a particular conception of life's meaning but also an account of why this counts as such, then Nietzsche's smashing of idols cannot help but appear nihilistic. In particular, Nietzsche's anti-realism, his denial of facts and a true world, seems to convey this. But he does not make innovative anti-realistic claims; he merely takes for granted that realist claims have been refuted in philosophy. Where he innovates is the next step: insofar as nothing is objective, then the values that otherwise would operate to support the normative authority and objectivity of life's goals (the realization of these values) become "devalued." The real danger, as Nietzsche sees it, comes when the authority of life's values depends on an objectivity that can no longer be sustained. Nietzsche's great innovation came when he authored an alternative in the suggestion that this situation need not devolve into nihilism, but not because he will reassert realism; he will instead posit new values, a new kind of hope that does not depend on objectivity to serve life.

In an interesting play on the motif of the second coming of Christ, but intended with the exact opposite effect, Nietzsche heralds the arrival of the Antichrist as the only bringer of hope in the face of Christian devaluing:

> This man of the future will redeem us not just from the
> ideal held up till now, but also from the things *which will
> have to arise from it*, from the great nausea, the will to
> nothingness, from nihilism, that stroke of midday and of
> great decision which makes the will free again, which gives
> earth its purpose and man his hope again, this Antichrist
> and anti-nihilist, this conqueror of God and of
> nothingness—*he must come one day* . . . .[40]

It is crucial to notice that Nietzsche still has a gospel he is proclaiming; it is replete with hope and striving, with salvation and new life. The old (Christian) salvation, he thinks, leads only to the degradation of life. Therefore, the death of God is not the high point of his gospel, but is its first word. The good news is not that God is dead but that the death of God need not signal the end of human existence, morality, or pronounce the fate of the world. In a sense, the part of Zarathustra's news that announces the death of God is merely old news: "have you not yet heard?" The people need to be told it to establish the ground for what comes after it. But they should not mourn the death of God since God's death does not signal the loss of meaning to life.[41] God's death, in fact, is the prerequisite to discovering genuine meaning and so long as the people continue to locate meaning in the "otherworldly hopes" God denotes, they will be kept from life's true meaning— the *Übermensch* himself.

The *Übermensch* is a manifestly ethical existence, a style of living in the face of devastated realities. "Thou shalt" is the form of the ethic the *Übermensch* must overcome by instead asserting, "I will." In one of Zarathustra's parables, the moral values represented by "thou shalt" are declared by the dragon (the strength the *Übermensch*, depicted as a lion, must fight) to be thousands of years old and therefore unshakable. "All value of all things shines on me. All value has long been created and I am all created value. Verily, there shall be no more 'I will'." But, of course, Zarathustra prizes the creation of new values. This involves the destruction of the dragon who asserts that there can be no new values since all values are already extant and reside with the dragon who is himself value. The lion preys on the old dragons by self-consciously identifying the illusion of created values. But the story cannot consummate with the victory of the lion. Zarathustra says the lion must become a child. The opposition to old values is not a sufficient project for the emergence of the *Übermensch* since, like a child, he will finally create out of sheer innocence. His new creations will not self-consciously fill the voids left by a moral situation devoid of old morals, but will emerge only as a function of a new freedom in which the past is not just overcome, but is now completely forgotten in the purity revisited upon the child. In other words, the new way of life for a world come of age in which the God of morality is dead along with the historic morality predicated upon that God must surpass the limited possibilities afforded it by the vacancies newly opened up. The struggles it must will for its exercise of the will to power must be ever new if the new way of life is to be characterized by motion.

A great deal, it must be admitted, turns on whether Nietzsche is successful in accomplishing this project or whether it is just a trophy to his good intentions. If postmodernity is merely the reverse side of modernity ("anti-modernity"), proceeding only by negation and denial of what comes before, then it can never be "more" than modernity; this is an observation accepted by those who instead prefer to name our philosophical and cultural situation as hyper-modern. Is the death of God, and therefore the loss of meaning granted to history by Christianity and German idealism, an extension of modernity's aspirations or something genuinely new? Does it exceed modernity's methods or merely signal their maturation while ultimately failing to surpass them? If Nietzsche is right, modernity is merely the anxiety produced by conflicting powers: taking leave of God but constantly assailed by the uncertain demands of living without the benign meaning God provides, finding instead God-like meaning in other God-like things—idols. This tension yields an unstable interval that unfolds in a variety of ways but whose variety is only a chimera masking the disquiet and the idols' largely unchecked reign. Despite its grandiose rhetoric, destroying idols does not properly feature among the practices of modernity; any destroying it undertakes is only half-hearted, supplanted by desperate and often dangerous efforts to forestall the complete destruction Nietzsche assigns to himself. Modernity fills the interval by deferring the inevitable while insisting in increasingly shrill tones that the idols are real, an insistence that raises the stakes of reason's dominance with violence. The deformed gods of modernity, in their unreality, struggle to elicit a loyalty that would only evaporate in the face of stronger wills. And so if Nietzsche too is only hyper-modern, then he has surely failed.

Therefore, we need to ask about Nietzsche's positive program and not just his negative one. What is the future that both partially exists for the *Übermensch* and is partially ushered in by him? Despite his exaltation of the childlike new way of life, Nietzsche writes only haltingly and hesitantly about what it consists in. At times, he seems only able to proceed by negation, by telling us what the *Übermensch* will *not* be like. This is why his account of the last man is more colorful and detailed. Perhaps there is an ironic or even absurd reason that lives of blithe resignation are more interesting than lives of vigorous activity. In particular, we must ask whether and how Nietzsche's positive orientation may benefit

Christianity's own positive project and professed positive existence while discerning some advantage, even appropriate chastisement and clarification, in his otherwise flawed genealogies. The following chapter will address these questions in more detail by way of a pair of idols Nietzsche names: the state and morality.

Chapter 5

Un-powering the good

Nietzsche is rarely viewed as a resource for thinking about politics in a constructive manner. One reason is that he seemed to refer to himself as a non-political thinker; but the main reason is that he is notoriously associated with the German ideology that transformed cultural critique into the political movement of National Socialism. It may therefore be of little use defending Nietzsche against the egregious use to which he was put, especially by the Nazis and by Mussolini. Indeed, even before these leaders, writers were beginning to expound Nietzsche's ideas in dangerous directions. In 1915, John Neville Figgis delivered one of the earliest extended theological engagements with Nietzsche, suggesting that the latter must be held responsible for the dangers inherent in his own thought even though they may not have been intended.[1] Commentators had already begun claiming to find themselves and their cultures in Nietzsche's descriptions of the *Übermensch*; others were developing social philosophies that traded in more deeply entrenched divisions between masters and slaves, rich and poor. We may suspect that such use only confirms the proclivities of the herd especially in their refusal to include themselves among the meandering coterie since those who learn of the *Übermensch* may too readily think that they are he (and which is a reason Nietzsche insisted that his descriptions were directed toward the future). Nietzsche may have been right in this regard, but his vindication is little consolation to those oppressed by risks Nietzsche took to prove himself right. "In any case," Figgis argues, "Nietzsche is guilty of them unless he took pains to avoid them."[2] How might any determined revolutionaries restrain themselves from the possibility of affording to themselves and their causes the slogan "beyond good and evil"? How, in other words, are they to keep from becoming indistinguishable from propounding nihilism itself?

Nietzsche was certainly an ancestor to an emerging fascist ideology. Yet among the ways that he differs from it, one in particular stands out for our purposes. In *The Politics of Cultural Despair*, Fritz Stern chronicles the ascendancy of the "Germanic ideology" through three different thinkers who, while not well known outside of German intellectual circles, nevertheless played important roles in a bourgeoning and ominous politics.[3] All shared critiques of modernity, democracy, and liberalism which they adduced, in most cases, independently of and prior to Nietzsche. The resort to such critiques was time-bound; the critiques took their form partly from what these thinkers perceived to be an enervating movement of conurbation with the attendant loss of traditional life and rural skill that made culture truly great. Separated from the traditional practices that formerly gave shape to the intellectual life of Germany, that life was now in danger of floating free on modern claims about the rationality of culture and the material edifices of industry. The "cultural Luddites," the great smashers of the machinery of modern culture, portended a conservative revolution that placed the blame of all contemporary ills on modernity and liberalism.

It is true that Nietzsche resembles these revolutionaries in some respects. But unlike them, Nietzsche was not driven by resentment nor by a nostalgia for a forgotten past. Both of these aspects served to propel the cultural criticism of these revolutionaries into a full-fledged political philosophy (though still quite vague in its particulars). Recalling Figgis, however, the point for us cannot be to vindicate Nietzsche but only to clarify the nature of any misunderstandings despite the extent to which Nietzsche's own writings may have invited them. A detailed account of this question is certainly beyond the scope of this book and is not immediately germane to my aims in it. Still, it is worth considering how Nietzsche came to be considered a dangerous political thinker when he never intended to be read politically. I think it is likely that, in cases where his thought becomes politically dangerous, Nietzsche's critiques of statist politics are disregarded and his social philosophy is facilely joined to already existing official political structures, or so I will contend.

The way that Nietzsche targets the state is one consequence of his extreme distrust of appeals to metaphysics. Like the grandness of anything that can claim metaphysical status—whether theories of knowledge over actual knowledge or moral theory over action—the state too authorizes itself metaphysically and so seizes more than its share of supremacy, or at least more than is warranted by the empirical reality of the people who comprise it and who therefore constitute a thoroughly abbreviated reach of authority. Its doing of these things, its overreaching, for Nietzsche, betrays its dishonesty as a form of lying; it is also the basis for how the state steals our loyalties. In this way, we may say that loyalty to the state manifests a modern secular anxiety that occupies the interval between the death of God and the letting go of God that modernity (and perhaps postmodernity) names. So to the extent that the state allegedly becomes the locus of Nietzsche's positive philosophy (as with National Socialism), it does so in disregard of the fact that its doing so *as a state* makes it subject to Nietzsche's twin accusations that it is both still wedded to modern forms of sovereignty and (therefore) perpetuates the slide toward nihilism or even gives rise to its fullest expression.

The demands the state places on its subjects makes the state into an idol insofar as the religious allegiances of a people are brought to bear on truly immanent and base objects like tax forms and governmental institutions through fantastically exalted images of military victory and declarations of authority that are nearly (or actually) divine in their rhetoric.[4] The state exclaims of itself, "On earth there is nothing greater than I: the ordering finger of God am I."[5] The "new idol," as Zarathustra calls the state, is more powerful than God in its ability to amass a loyalty at the far end of which is *treason*—and loss of the only identity that matters—rather than *blasphemy*, the old-fashioned betrayal of the gods of actual people before they (the gods and the peoples) were subdued. The state is also an idol in a further, more insidious respect—it demands sacrifice.

On one level, it is obvious that the state does not exist in the same way that government buildings, bureaucrats, and tax forms exist—these have tangible existence and are nevertheless among the ways that the state claims to exist. But if state *artifacts* exist in an obvious fashion, why not conclude that they are *all* that exist? Governmental rendering of their domains in ways that coincide with their dominion (such as geographic regions divided according to local tax rates) are enlisted in actual claims to authority. These cases can be condensed to this logic: we can tax you because "we" exist and "you" are represented on our tax maps—this is how we know we have the right to tax and how we know you are subject to us in this regard. Those things that are primary (that is, that obviously exist) are only the maps and the people who are being addressed; everything else is just an idol whose existence owes to the fears that lead people to make metaphysical claims. At least this is how Nietzsche thought about the state. For subsequent Nietzscheans like Foucault, this means that the state is an "epiphenomenon" having an existence that is only skin deep even though few are willing to risk the consequences of scratching through the surface.

If Christian politics is entitled to be non-statist or anti-statist, it is so, on the basis of the confession that, despite the new idol, God still rules the cosmos and demands no more sacrifices. God's purposes for creation do not ultimately depend on states, on their ability to marshal forces against the enemies of order, on their efforts at constraining injustice. It is true that the new idol got its ideas from Christian rulers only subsequently to supplant them through updated reasons for their existence. While Christian political thought has not spoken with a unified voice on the nature of political power, it has always relativized political authority in light of God's judgment in a way that it is possible to argue along with Nietzsche that, while not free of metaphysics in the way he supposes, Christianity does not identify the state as the locus of true virtue, political or otherwise. In doing so, we are following Nietzsche's critique of the state; his positive political contribution will be taken up in the following chapter.

One example of how Christian political theology relativizes political authority can be seen in Thomas Aquinas. While Aquinas was certainly not what any modern commentator would call a "non-statist" thinker (even granting the anachronism), he radically relativizes the civil government by subjecting it to God's ordering and judgment. In one respect, he quintessentially embodies the kind of metaphysical approach Nietzsche opposes. But Aquinas is also typical of Christian thinking that may, in other respects, profit from and extend Nietzsche's critiques of the modern state. According to Aquinas, kings must depend on the relativization of their authority to be virtuous Christian kings; that is, they will themselves acquire the right affective virtues by reflecting on how their own government is analogous to how God governs the universe.[6] The knowledge that their government is *merely* analogous to God's government will be the source of their gentleness and justice. In exercising analogous political authority, it is not up to kings to govern with the final end—beatitude and friendship with God—in mind even though they are responsible for directing the civil community toward the more modest end of virtuous living; human laws ("positive law") ought to promote this. Nevertheless, Aquinas notes that the ultimate end of virtuous living is nothing other than beatitude itself, though this can only be brought by God and as such, it is not the responsibility of human government. But somehow human government should still, in Aquinas's words, "command those things which lead to the happiness of Heaven," and forbid the contrary.

Why does there seem to be confusion regarding the role of human governments in generating virtuous people? It could be that Aquinas does not finally want to distinguish carefully between the natural, temporal ends and the final, theological ends of human community. The former take their cues from the latter, being reflected as pale imitations, notable in their yearning and incompleteness. There cannot be a sharp division of labor between the king and priest. A good and just ruler promotes those provisional goods that are in service to the goods of the church. This is why Aquinas contends that all kings must be subject to the Pope.

At this point, we can again acknowledge that we speak anachronistically when we take kings to be stand-ins for the modern state since, if anything, the reverse is really the case. Nietzsche's suspicion of state idolatry is not immediately connected to the ways that Christian rulers may have buttressed their claims to sovereignty. It is a suspicion of the political void left behind once such sovereignty no longer succeeds in demanding the loyalty of the sovereign's subjects. The state is a modern invention that follows in this wake. As such, it must position itself as a self-proclaimed unifier by enveloping all the elements within its reach. It says, "I am the people," something that Nietzsche takes to be a manifest lie. It nevertheless ascribes to itself the ultimacy that he surely thought Christian kings enjoyed by direct appeal to divine mandate even though Christian thought has generally made this point with a good deal more nuance.

Even so, if the promotion of civic virtue is conceived in Christian kingship as Aquinas describes, what is there to say about the civic virtue that states are in the position to promote? For all his contemptuous language about virtue, Nietzsche after all was actually keenly concerned with the question of virtue. What is the culture of the last man if not a culture totally bereft of virtue? And that culture's inability to recognize its own sorry state owes preeminently to its lack of virtue since, out of ignorance, it thinks its most egregious vices are really virtues.[7] When Nietzsche challenges virtue, it is precisely because he is challenging the culture of the last man. And so the question of civic virtue remains, though what has changed in the transition from Christian rulers to the modern state is the new normativity of the secular. Nietzsche's entire project is almost certainly a grand preoccupation with the production of modern virtue without reversion to those forces that birthed modernity in the first place, but by appealing to more ancient (pre-Christian, Greek) accounts of human existence.

A king's subjection to the Pope would not have pleased Nietzsche, who surely would not have seen much difference between a king and a Pope.[8] But for Christian political thought, it raises a parallel question to Nietzsche's: What about secular rulers? It is not clear that Aquinas, for example, allowed for a "virtuous" king who does not worship God (nor did Augustine). Such a king could not display real virtue since his virtues would be ordered toward the wrong end, which is precisely why, more generally, Christian virtue cannot be the same as antique virtue; they cannot share the same end or *telos*. Indeed, such a king would not be likely to subject himself to the Pope, and he could only ratify laws that would make his subjects relatively good rather than simply good (that is, people would only become "good according to the regime"). In such a case, Christians are still subject to the king but are not required to obey his laws, particularly if the laws contradict virtue or divine justice. Aquinas seems to have changed his mind slightly as to whether this kind of king ought to be deposed (or killed) or simply endured. In the *Commentary on the Sentences* (1254–1256), he writes that "one who liberates his country by killing a tyrant [who had been installed by force] is to be praised and rewarded." But writing to the king of Cyprus a decade later, he is understandably more chastened, claiming that it is more Christian to endure suffering under unjust rulers as the martyrs did under Roman emperors.[9] If rulers are to be opposed at all, it should not be done by private people taking their initiative to kill the king, since this may only make matters worse for the society as a whole. In some cases, Christian subjects will not only have the right to disobey a tyrannical ruler and laws contrary to virtue, but they will be obligated to disobedience. However, this will not hold for *everything* a bad ruler commands of his subjects since some cases will be less straightforward and subjects may or may not choose to obey, though Aquinas urges Christians to forego their right to disobey, especially if this would cause a scandal. Instead, they should, as it were, go the extra mile.

It seems to me that there is more than a family resemblance between the Christian response to an unjust king and to the new idol of the state that makes Aquinas a suitable interlocutor with Nietzsche at this juncture, however else we might want to identify their vast differences. Christians, that is to say, are quite a lot like Nietzsche's "people" whose virtue enables them to resist the state's lies. In the same way that herd morality ceases to be moral apart from the life of the herd—in this case, the state's "people"—the worth of the herd necessarily determines the value of the morality it both produces and on which it depends. But because the state tells a lie when it says, "I am the people," it fails to be worthy of the morality it discharges as normative for life within it. It cannot deliver on its promise to bring happiness, but instead, like idols of stone that cannot speak (let alone change the fates of the ones that worship them), it is powerless to fulfill the true longings of the people. In fact, it is worse than this: the state positively seeks to enslave.

Early in his writings, Nietzsche identified the way that the very existence of language gives the lie to claims that there are universal moral codes. In his mature works (notably *BGE* and *GM*), he treats this theme under the obviously moral nomenclature of "good" and "evil," where he argues that such words purport to speak of a grand universality when, in fact, they are only cover-up concepts for resentment. In similar fashion, the state lies when it refuses to admit to the particularity of every moral language since its own claim to power partially resides in monolingual declarations meant to apply to everyone, especially to its neighbors over which it wishes to claim moral authority. If the state were to acknowledge that its neighbors may not understand the moral discourse of its own people, it would no longer possess the marks of a state but only the feeble (relatively speaking) authority of a people.[10]

In one respect, this is merely a reappearance of Nietzsche's perspectivism cast in a moral rather than epistemological mode. The appearance of the world (setting aside, as we often must do with Nietzsche, the question of the status of the "real" world) changes with the linguistic sources brought to bear on the activity of perceiving. What we call a thing and how we talk about it in the context of some activities and not others not only indicate what we think about a thing but also partially determine our capacity for even noticing it to begin with. These comments about the state, however, are perspectivism inflected in a way that takes the state as a metaphysical entity that only bears a clumsily despotic (because lying) relation to the people that comprise it. Even though Nietzsche is not known as a political thinker—indeed, he called himself "the last unpolitical German"[11]—others have clearly developed his thought in a more explicitly political direction. Still, the tradition of reading Nietzsche as apolitical based on this comment owes largely to Thomas Mann for whom Nietzsche was a kind of conservative romantic. According to Peter Bergmann, Mann's sentiment was based on a mistranslation (or led to a mistranslation) that, if properly rendered into English, would have made Nietzsche the last *antipolitical* German.[12] Nietzsche was antipolitical by taking a position of culture that put it, in practical terms, at odds with the state. The separation of culture from the state, however, should not be taken to mean that culture is unpolitical except in terms that give true politics over to the exclusive domain of sovereign power. In this, there is both a critique of the uncultured life of politics as it had come normally to be conceived and also of the preference for the "politics" of culture over against the corrupt politics of the state—corrupted precisely in its rejection of culture.[13]

Nietzsche's Zarathustra preached a communal gospel in which the common ambition to produce the *Übermensch* elicits the best qualities of a people, those things we can only rightly call political—though social rather than governmental. The focused energies that are required for this will drive solitary individuals from their complacent repose in otherworldly hopes and transcendent dreams, engaging them on a terrestrial surface, employing their skills for a momentous present pregnant with a future of meaning and, therefore, itself meaningful. If the saintly hermit encountered by Zarathustra in that work's Prologue was content to be alone with the animals and his songs to God, it was because he did not yet know that God is dead—he was therefore kept from seeing that his songs are quite meaningless. What the hermit took as an isolation oriented toward communion with God is, for Zarathustra, nothing other than a refusal of human politics.[14]

Nietzsche does not despair to the extent that he refuses to equate the state with the people. "While there is still a people," Zarathustra says, "it does not understand the state."[15] There will always be a place for the politics of culture that is greater than the limited account of the political on which the state depends so long as the state persists in offering an account of its sovereignty that is antithetical to the cultural life of the nation. A people may be powerless to the state but there will always be those aspects that still contribute to the shape of their common life apart from the state's exercise of power; the people's relative powerlessness, then, is no reason to refrain from describing these aspects as political. Taking the thought to the extreme, we may therefore inquire into the *nature* of the state and whether there is such a thing. This question, for Christian thought, will split into two considerations: whether and how secular rule relates to the human ends of beatitude and friendship with God even while such rule does not pursue these ends; and whether and how the politics of a people who continue to pursue beatitude and friendship with God relates to sovereign authority that does not, that is (anachronistically), how the church relates to the state. But what, for Nietzsche, constitutes a people? He holds out for a people who are not fooled by the seductions of the state, even and especially in its demand for sacrifice. This is a people who do not yet exist except in Zarathustra's exhortations. It is a future community that does not rely on sovereign power or the state's lying moral claims to know how to live.

In this way, Nietzsche differs from the conservative, revolutionary precursors to the Nazis that Stern investigates. For them, the key historical moments were always in the past. The uncertainties of the nineteenth century that started to become apparent once the cultural reality of the death of God was comprehended were too much for them. Unlike Nietzsche, they could not envision how life might still be lived in a post-Christian, liberal ethos. Recalling Nietzsche's critique of those who had an undue fascination with the past, it is clear that these conservative revolutionaries did not have the courage Nietzsche thought necessary to accept the *Übermensch* as a future reality. There is bitter truth to Nietzsche's claim in this regard, especially as it touches his own biography. When his *Zarathustra* first appeared in print, he was astonished by the almost complete indifference it received and so he seems to have consoled himself with the thought that, like Zarathustra himself, he was too much ahead of his time. In 50 years, he would claim to others, his name would be famous throughout Europe; perhaps chairs would be established for the interpretation of Zarathustra:

> But it would be a complete contradiction of myself if
> I expected ears *and hands* for *my* truths already today: that
> I am not heard today, that no one today knows how to take
> from me, is not only comprehensible; it even seems to me
> right [16]

Yet Nietzsche is not here conceding a belief in the inevitable progress of history as at least one commentator supposes. [17] Instead, the future holds, even for the fate of Nietzsche's works themselves, nothing more certain than the empirical possibility of a new kind of people. This is also Nietzsche's greatest hope against the state's dogged influence on a people's identity and constitution. The community of the *Übermensch* will be one that, in its very production of the *Übermensch*, has been able to overcome the forces of conformity from the world. Such a production signals the end of the state, not only because it has been supplanted by a more determinative social body—the *Übermensch* and his creators—but also because no state can survive without a critical mass of its populace giving itself over to the life of the state, something the

Übermensch will not do. The state thus ends in two respects. It is exposed as a fraud, its pretentious claims to unsurpassed existential value and moral normativity shown for what they are, namely, desperate attempts to shore up power. But the state also ends in respect of its abandonment to a privative existence in the wake of the emergence of the *Übermensch* and his new society such that the end of the state is actually equated with the rise of the *Übermensch*, not just its condition of possibility.

When the state ends, the need for herd morality (herd *virtue*) ends as well. In its place, Nietzsche envisions a boundlessly creative people who embrace an authentic existence and for whom creativity rather than morality is a first principle. In fact, morality only *appeared* to be a first principle of the state when all along it was the insecure assertion of impotent power. The community of the *Übermensch*, however, does not submit to the brood's conformity, releasing the embracers of life to a "not superfluous" existence: "there begins the song of necessity, the unique and inimitable tune."[18]

There is here the boundless, antinomian note one frequently descries in Nietzsche's ecstatic rhetoric. Nonetheless, even the *Übermensch* is not actually amoral, just as he is not devoid of virtue; in this sense, Christian virtue is no less creative, though Nietzsche must have thought so.[19] Consider the role similar virtues play in Aquinas's provision for overriding the strict letter of the law (positive human law) if danger is imminent. This is not usually a judgment for private individuals but for governing authorities, though Aquinas goes on to comment that, in an emergency, an individual can help himself to another's property and this is not considered stealing. We are to assume that knowing what constitutes an emergency, knowing when to override the law, and to what extent to do so are all matters of practical reason conditioned by the virtues. And since positive law is meant to engender virtue, it has the ironic effect of stimulating those very qualities through observance that will determine when one ought to break with observance. In other words, what makes the breaking of a law just rather than unjust depends on the prior effectiveness of an obeyed law for bringing about the virtues necessary to break it. This is not the case with unjust laws, but with just laws that cannot allow for every hard case and emergency simply because they are laws.

Unjust laws, though, may slip by unnoticed in a society that is insufficiently virtuous. If a preponderance of unjust laws go by unnoticed, the people will be formed by observing them, meaning that they will be formed according to unjust custom, losing the ability to recognize manifold injustices. Tyrannical laws form unjust people who can then no longer recognize tyranny in any form. However, Aquinas insists that all the while the laws will be thought of as making people good, though they will only be making people relatively good. By another measure, they will easily be seen as corrupt, made in the image of the values that dominate the society in which law-making and virtue-making go unchecked insofar as laws and semblances of virtues rise and fall together. However, "relatively good" is not good enough since it leaves a tyrannical ruler to unquestioned and unchallenged tyranny. The ability for a society to recognize whether a ruler is just or not will rather depend on the presence of those who are not just "relatively good" but "simply good." A "simply good" people have virtues formed by something other than the corrupt laws of the community. They have divine law, the law of Christ. Such laws are not opposed to natural law but, since recognition of natural law is impaired by sin, the addition of divine law does not just add but also *repairs*. The purpose of human community is simple goodness. In those communities constituted by relative goodness and semblances of virtue, natural law is not sufficient to curb that community's own excesses.

Even more than Nietzsche's "people" who resist the state, all of this makes clear why Aquinas thinks the temporal order actually needs the church. And it goes without saying that, to do so, the church must at points resist the temporal order. The hierarchy of the church over the state is not a matter of domination, but of ordering (though the very existence of "church" as separate from "world" owes to the Fall). The state needs the church, not for the church to rule over the state, but for the church to exemplify simple goodness in human communities marked by relative goodness. The flattening of hierarchy that came with later theologies often converted the relationship of church and state into two separate spheres with different ends. But Aquinas is clear: the ends of the church are the same as the ends of the state since there is only one end for all of humankind: beatitude and friendship with God.[20]

We turn now to a closely related idol. Nietzsche associated morality with the state such that once state idolatry is exposed, the people who formerly submitted to it will likewise be liberated from state morality. As a writer "beyond good and evil," Nietzsche sought to purge these evaluative words of their moralistic qualities. What is good? Everything that heightens the feeling of power in man, the will to power, power itself. What is bad? Everything that is born of weakness.[21] Amidst his efforts to disclaim all teleology, one usually finds Nietzsche beginning with pluralistic notions that have by now become widely accepted. His difficulty is not first with the notion of goals that give rise to morality, but with the fact that there is simply a multitude of goals. The well-traveled Zarathustra "discovered the good and evil of many peoples. And [he] found no greater power on earth than good and evil." But one people's good was sometimes another people's evil. "Much I found called evil here, and decked out with purple honors there."[22] What is universal, though, is the exaltation of "good" and condemnation of "evil." We may identify the parallel concept of *synderesis* in medieval moral theology which enjoins "do good and avoid evil." The content of those terms, though, is not elaborated on the level of rational principle but by the faculty of *conscience* that operates in particular situations. The point of this separation in the medieval inheritance is to account for the fact that nearly every human agent will describe their actions as good, leading moral theologians like Aquinas to call synderesis a natural faculty of the reason.

However, Nietzsche is no simple pluralist, content to expose the fact that there are as many moralities as there are peoples. Instead, he goes much further in questioning the very suitability of morality to humanity, especially once all metaphysical crutches are abandoned. Our language is shot through with teleological assumptions that are not immediately thought of as moral, though Nietzsche includes them in his polemic. "Healthy," for example, implies an ideal state for anything that it describes. Nietzsche does not just reject this ideal, as though he favors illness over health, but the very categorical schema. In the same way, he necessarily abjures all rationalistic explanations of morality, as we described earlier, particularly those accounts that attempt to grant for themselves a scientific basis: morality as a science. And while philosophers argue about who has accomplished this most successfully, Nietzsche notices that no one seems to be questioning the very idea of morality itself.

> What philosophers called "the rational ground of morality" and sought to furnish was, viewed in the proper light, only a scholarly form of *faith* in the prevailing morality, a new way of *expressing* it, and thus itself a fact within a certain morality, indeed even in the last resort a kind of denial that this morality *ought* to be conceived as a problem—and in any event the opposite of a testing, analysis, doubting and vivisection of this faith.[23]

Nietzsche is claiming that what kept philosophers from questioning the very idea of morality was not their success in finding rational foundations for their moral schemes—though they did claim to find them—but their lack of will to subject to scrutiny the morality of the powerful which included themselves.

This is a more sophisticated form of the traditional *argumentum ad hominem* where the decisive factor in the genealogy is the *interest* of the philosopher in maintaining the status quo regardless of the rationality of their philosophical program. In this, Nietzsche resembles Marx and other critics of ideology. For example, however impressed Nietzsche may or may not be with Kant's categorical imperative, he still thinks that it is fair to ask what it tells us about the person who claims that the categorical imperative is a universal. In Kant's case, perhaps it tells us that Kant is the kind of person who knows how to obey and thinks others should be too. (In *GM*, written around the same time, Nietzsche critiques ascetic priests for parallel reasons, their subjugation of their own desires bearing witness to their desire to control everything else, especially those things outside of their control.[24]) The problem with Kant, of course, is that he is not well traveled like Zarathustra; in fact, it is said that he never left his hometown which can make one suspect with Nietzsche that Kant's morality was just a universal by projection.

We therefore might suppose that Christian morality only falls under Nietzsche's critique insofar as it purports to be rational, which is to say, insofar as it is attainable by every thinking person simply through the exercise of their reason. And as a critic of the Enlightenment exaltation of rationality—a preeminently Apollonian seduction—this is certainly the case. To be sure, there are many moralities but Nietzsche does not think this necessarily means anything beyond the simple observation that there *are* many moralities. After all, one cannot directly move from the observation that there are many moralities to the conclusion that morality therefore lacks a rational foundation. It may lack such a foundation, but then again, there may also be a rational account of the multiplicity of moralities. But Nietzsche is suspicious of meta-level postulates that attempt to account for this plurality in the same way that he was suspicious of the ways that theories of knowledge supervene on knowledge itself. Meta-level postulates that serve a regulative function are not themselves moral codes or anything else moral at all; they are evidence of anxiety over moral truth. But Nietzsche does not think we should have any stake in moral truth for the same reason that we should not have any stake in epistemological truth: truth and falsity correspond to elements in rational discourse that are always insufficient reasons for either abandoning or adopting morality or knowledge.

Nietzsche does not mean by this that morality is irrational nor that what is immoral is better than what is moral. Both of these judgments would still only take for granted the ascendancy of reason. The former judgment (that morality is irrational) suggests that the quality of rationality is material to morality, whereas this is precisely something Nietzsche opposes. Morality can be neither rational nor irrational since it operates on an entirely different plane, one more honest and closer to the exercise of life than reason's verdicts. Kant, Hume, Diderot, and the others would have been more honest had they admitted that their project was not one of proffering moralities and so of heightening their disagreements, but of *justifying* the Christian morality that they all generally took for granted.[25] Their views on marriage, promise-making and keeping, and justice are not remarkable in how they differ but in how they do not. The debate about their difference was only, in Nietzsche's polemic, a ruse for their inability or their refusal to subject to scrutiny the vast moral tradition they all seemed to accept without argument.

Likewise, the latter judgment (that immorality is better than morality) suggests that morality submits to a more fundamental criterion according to which we can rationally decide which is better. Here, Nietzsche thinks we ought to conceive of morality as a way of life that can be identified by its practices rather than a set of ideas. Once, therefore, correspondence theories of truth have been expunged, the thought that moral ideas have a referent in the world that is somehow less important than the ideas (about which we can theorize) disappears. What is left over, Nietzsche hopes, is actual living that may be discussed but will always be insufficiently captured by discussion and theory. Put simply, if morality is practice, the question of truth becomes a second-order question at best since no practice can be truer than its exercise.

One way this move was disguised in the name of rationality was through appeals to human nature as such, a concept that was thought to yield a foundation for delineating moral rules. Since human nature is obviously shared by all humans, and because rationality is a trait intrinsic to being human, then, if done correctly, any resulting morality could claim universality. Some such attempts were made by connecting the passions with morality, but still follow the same pattern of rooting the argument in human nature as such. There are two things to notice about this strategy. First, these are arguments always at least one-step removed from the *content* of morality since they trade on the philosophy's ability to *justify* what is moral in one way or another rather than elaborate a form of life. Second, any appeal to human nature as such will entail an implicit appeal to teleology: what humans are *for*, in this case. For Nietzsche, this is an appeal to theology when it entails a metaphysics of the human person or of human community from which ends for living are derived. In this, he was certainly correct and, as in other aspects of his thought, the critique is not primarily against the fact of appeals to ends (is not the *Übermensch* the noble human end?) but against the guise under which such ends are suppressed.

The danger of lying to yourself to suppress something is that you will only be able to carry on if you are so successful in your lying that you believe your own lies to be true (after all, every lie parades itself as true and in lying to yourself, there is no room for awareness of the fact of the lie to be maintained). Therefore, the suppression of human ends in thinking about morality led inexorably to the *rejection of the notion* of human ends as requisite for the intelligibility of morality. What is left, therefore, is the "as such" status of concepts like human nature.[26] Without ends, the reason can only function as a calculator, assessing means or adding up units of utility and pleasure.[27]

This explains why Nietzsche's gripe is with philosophers rather than with the proverbial plain person. Philosophers are more likely to fall victim to falsehoods since the excesses of their enterprise seem to encourage sophisticated ways of simply recasting a philosopher's prejudices in ways rendered universal because rational. Therefore, it is one thing to point out that rationality is not universal—that, like moralities, there are many rationalities—but it is another thing to expose the philosophical propensity for the craven disguise of prejudice. Philosophical attempts to lay down basic truths are only the display of an uncritically cherished darling: "while what happens at bottom is that a prejudice, a notion, an 'inspiration,' generally a desire of the heart sifted and made abstract, is defended by them with reasons sought after the event."[28] Defending something after the fact is not to be avoided in principle; but it is *disingenuous* when its execution cloaks the fact that it is truly after and not before. After all, philosophers trade in the *a priori*; everything else is sociology or psychology.[29]

We have already covered some of this ground under earlier headings such as "knowledge" but there is an additional element to Nietzsche's specific attack on Christianity. His most trenchant critique of Christian morality proceeds from a genealogical account in which the story is cast as a kind of slave revolt. And, we may add, this critique of Christian *morality* is his most sustained and comprehensive attack on Christianity itself. For all the pluralism in morality that exists among different peoples, Nietzsche divines two basic traits or classes, which he calls *master morality* and *slave morality*. He has no quarrels with "good" in its original meaning, prior to the corruption of slaves who reverse its meaning out of their resentment. Originally, "good" is merely the self-description of the powerful in their exercise of power. "Evil" appears when those who endure that power attach moral language to their feeling of powerlessness and project that language back onto those who were formerly good in a straightforward sense.[30] Evil is therefore an invention of slaves for enacting moral revenge against the masters and, over time, the elaborate edifice of slave morality obscures its origins and represses its elemental ambition— the desire for retribution among those who are weak and do not share in the benefits of cultural ascendancy.

For Nietzsche, the Sermon on the Mount is the *tour de force* of slave morality. How, he asks, did we ever come to think that being meek is virtuous? According to his genealogy, meekness was revalued as a positive virtue by the meek themselves when they could neither succeed in a world of assertive souls nor achieve revenge for their lack of success in any other way than demonizing their opponents and exalting their own feeble state. Now, not only are the meek "good" but they shall inherit the earth as well. The deferral of judgment on the enemies of the meek is only an instance of appeals to transcendence that Nietzsche faults for discharging our moral confusion and resignation. Thus insofar as the meek are good on account of their successful campaign to revalue morality in their favor, they are also partakers of revenge for how they have waged their campaign. Still, Zarathustra counsels that "a little revenge is more human than no revenge," which itself suggests its own morality, one that makes every attempt to be human, natural, and faithful to the earth.[31]

On this basis, the reason slave morality is abhorrent to Nietzsche cannot be because of the element of revenge.[32] The noble and the weak both seek vengeance when wronged and this is primarily just a comment about the way things are at the level of observation. The difference is that in the weak, the desire for revenge festers, breeding resentment as a deep-seated aspect of their disposition, infecting the character and eventually giving rise to a whole new set of values. The noble seek their revenge and move on; in this way, they overcome the wrongs done to them and those who did the wrongs.

What Nietzsche finds praiseworthy in the noble, then, is not their vengeance, but their ability to keep the wrongs they suffer from prevailing over them (as we noted earlier, it allows them to "forgive"). Master morality is not a program for retribution, but a positive way of life that is itself so compelling that it is not easily distracted. Zarathustra reproaches those who, though deep, also wound deeply, "suffer too deeply even from small wounds.... But beware lest it become your downfall that you suffer all their poisonous injustice."[33] The associations with Eternal Recurrence and tragedy are obvious. The critique of Christian morality is contrastive with pre-Homeric Greece that produced tragedy out of the courage to affirm life rather than to explain suffering, which is also the selfsame courage the *Übermensch* has for affirming the Eternal Recurrence and for exactly the same reasons. Yet even courage is not afforded a primary value in Nietzsche's account, but a way of life that is more basic than any salutary descriptions. Courage may *describe* that way of life, but it does not precede it or supervene on it in a regulative fashion. The same may be said for revenge; it also is a secondary description that finds its place in a whole way of life that, in its expression, may be either commendable or lamentable. The lamentable revenge of slave morality is therefore not a function of its vengeance but most likely of the way it corrupts any way of life that might have persisted without being overwhelmed. The creation of slave values corresponds to the destruction of freedom even though that creation must immediately be denied. This is the second reason Nietzsche disapproves of slave morality, that is, it is enlisted in deception: pretending to others and to oneself that one's morality is universal and has no contingent history. Genealogy is therefore cast as a truth-telling practice.

Why is telling the truth so important to Nietzsche? Utilitarians had their own reasons for commending telling the truth, but these very same reasons also are put in service of commending telling untruths. The famous example that asks whether you would lie to a murderer as to the whereabouts of a potential victim you are hiding is usually invoked to argue for lying on consequentialist grounds. But Nietzsche knew that such arguments could not sufficiently account for the will to truth, the desire not to be lied to. We will consider the will to truth in the following chapter. Yet if truth telling is the character of genealogy, we may rightly wonder whether it is possible to give a genealogical account of truth telling itself. Nietzsche did not attempt this, but Foucault later did.[34]

What Nietzsche wants is not so much *no* morality, but a morality that is almost impossible to imagine since it does not share the resentment that he thinks by now is deeply interwoven throughout all of our moral concepts. He wants a positive morality that is subordinated to free actions that in turn take their cues from the goals of the *Übermensch*; as moral concepts, perhaps they may be articulated after the fact as descriptions of actions ("I just did *this*") but they never play a regulative function ("thou shalt not"). The *Übermensch* knows what to do through the drives to reach goals and achieve, through his exercise of his will to power, which is always amoral.

The *Übermensch* is one of Nietzsche's celebrated free spirits for whom freedom is a positive activity of energetic living rather than a condition determined by the release of constraints. Zarathustra asks his disciples, "You call yourself free? Your dominant thought I want to hear, and not that you have escaped from a yoke." The entire question of yokes is immaterial. "Free *from* what? As if that mattered to Zarathustra! But your eyes should tell me brightly: free *for* what?"[35] Being free *from* is what Charles Taylor calls freedom as an "opportunity concept," a notion that makes reference to which opportunities are available once obstacles have been removed.[36] But on its own, freedom *from* does not say very much. It is a formal concept that is always at least one-step removed from the actions for which it purports to make room. Politically speaking, because there is nothing more important to modern liberal thought, it is vulnerable to the accusation that on its own it is not enough to sustain cultures and traditions. Of course, Zarathustra is speaking to creators of a cultural future for whom freedom *for* is the only freedom that matters. Taylor calls this kind of freedom an "exercise concept" because it can only be known and known to be possessed once you know what you want to do and as you actually do it—this is the life of the *Übermensch*.

It is probably impossible to generalize about the Christian moral tradition, but there is certainly room to include what is of value in Nietzsche's positive ethic of freedom. Nietzsche makes quick work of any subtleties Christian thought has attached to Jesus's teaching on the Law and the entire question of Law and gospel. For him, sons of God have no need of morality. "Jesus said to his Jews: 'The law was made for servants—love God as I love him, as his son! What have we sons of God to do with morality!' "[37] Yet, for the Christian, does this not ring true at least in part? The Pauline Law of the Spirit is certainly cast as both positive and free.

The Christian life is one of freedom that owes to the living nature of the Spirit, the Spirit of the risen and so living Christ. Christ is not a dispenser of a law but the living embodiment of law. As Albert Schweitzer said, "The essence of Christianity is world-affirmation which has gone through an experience of world-negation. In the eschatological world-view of world-negation, Jesus proclaims the ethic of active love."[38] Even the many negative commands in the Bible ("thou shalt not") are not merely prohibitive. There is a tradition of showing how, for example, the Ten Commandments are much more than the negative restrictions they appear to be. In reality, the Law establishes positive practices that extend much wider than the commands that seek to limit their exercise so that every commandment presupposes a positive practice that precedes it, and therefore makes it intelligible. Not committing adultery is more than a negative injunction in the way that it calls to mind and partially serves to shape the practice of marriage that gives the command intelligibility. In the same way, Zarathustra himself occasionally issues commands that resemble the ascetic life that Nietzsche elsewhere faults for an obsession with life-denial. "A free life is still free for great souls. Verily, whoever possesses little is possessed that much less: praised be a little poverty!"[39]

Nietzsche advocates a non-resentful, non-reactive ethic. His nomenclature of slave morality carries the inference that slaves only come to their conclusions about what is virtuous on account of their status as slaves. The ethic is defined by its opposition to the master. Once, however, they are freed from slavery, the absence of the master throws the coherence of the ethic into confusion. Political revolutions can display this disorder where every revolutionary tenet is set in exact opposition to the other regime until the revolution succeeds. Nietzsche wants spirits who are free *for*, who are animated by a goal (and so an ethic) that literally knows nothing of opposition, that has no enemies and so is indifferent to the presence of rivals. Enemies may oppose it, but their opposition does nothing to the way of life for these free spirits.

The Augustinian doctrine of privation yields an account of good and evil that intersects with this aspect of Nietzsche's genealogy. Good is non-reactive in exactly this way; it does not depend on the presence of evil or even on its existence since even if evil had not come to exist God would still be good. Moreover, goodness does not just make affinities on the logic that the enemy of my enemy is my friend.[40] It is not goodness that is reactive but evil since the latter has no positive existence, only "existing" through privation and absence of the good. Nietzsche, of course, conceived of evil quite differently. According to him, what we call evil is the indeterminacy of life characterized by chance (that is, tragedy) and the powerlessness of the weak to respond to it, existing at the mercy of the strong who overcome nature's tragedy. The moral response to such tragedy, for Nietzsche, must be one of unmitigated non-reactivity, though not because evil has been rendered ontologically privative in the way Augustine argues. The existence of evil (again, conceived as tragedy) must be accepted without question or any attempt to enlist evil in something that is good.[41]

In similar fashion, the difficulties that attend to the vocabulary of non-violence are well known for their implication that violence determines the nature of anything peaceful. Even though at the level of practice violence is easier to identify, Christian thought has sought ways of affirming the priority of peace, ontological and otherwise. Just as God would still be good even if there were no evil, God is eternally peace and peaceful in Trinitarian relations absolutely apart from the conflict that seems inevitably to mark human relations. For example, John Howard Yoder's is a positive ethic of peace in this regard in that he does not assume that violence names a discrete phenomenon or tendency, but only names the privative existence of non-peace. Because of the theological contention that peace admits to a deeper and fuller reality than violence (due to only the former having positive existence), there is no exact opposite to peace, no real rival; there are only glimpses of *lack* that always will point to the *more* of peace insofar as the positive good for human social relations, say, cannot be known or extrapolated from the negative realities of conflict and difference.

Nietzsche envisioned violence as part of a positive way of life disconnected from the violence one suffered, allowing him to evade the accusation that his is an ethic of resentment. But an ethic need not be associated with violence in this same way in order not to operate through resentment. As will be discussed in Chapter 6, this is a major point of contention among Christian thinkers who have sought to make use of Nietzsche while not tolerating his fundamental metaphysics of violence. For now, however, let us consider the respects in which a Christian ethic of peace may be a positive one. In an ethic of resentment, the conditions that pertain to the strong are taken for granted by everyone, especially the weak, although the weak ethic accepts these conditions only to revalue them by erecting their own ethic in direct opposition to the strong. There is no originality in this move, Nietzsche rightly charges, since the weak are entirely dependent on both the existence of the strong as well as their strong status, the former because the identity of the weak is increasingly wrapped up with the strong insofar as they are identified through reaction (*we* are *their* enemies) and the latter because without the strong status of the opposing party, the weak are not only not "weak," but are literally nothing.

This means that the weak are tempted to accept the terms and conditions of discourse put forth by the strong. And here the normativity of violence comes into view. For example, the refusal to take for granted the terms of debate established ahead of time by those who privilege positions of violence extends to critiques Yoder makes of liberation theologians who justify violent revolution. Their justification is that they are driven to violence by violent oppressors. But since this is a move of reaction, Yoder thinks it only entrenches the oppression further insofar as the *methods* of the oppressors still prevail even when the liberators come to power.

> To grant to the oppressor that he has the last word, that the alternatives as the oppressor sees them are the way they are, that there is no path of radical change which is not the chaos which the oppressor fears, that there is no step forward which does not wait for the oppressor to take it first, that his authority is genuinely a bulwark against total social collapse, is to have become intellectually, and therefore also emotionally and morally subservient to the oppressor, instead of appropriating and proclaiming that intellectual and moral liberation which must be the pre-condition of effective institutional liberty.[42]

While this is not a precise identification of an ethic of resentment, it does share Nietzsche's fundamental concern that any non-dominant (which usually means non-sovereign) way of life will generally make use of the opposing side, even while usually *reversing* it, and almost certainly disguising and denying that it is doing so. In time, it will have entirely forgotten that it has done so, inviting and depending on self-deception to be able then to say, "We have a positive way of life!"

As with so many aspects of Nietzsche's thought, then, there is the challenge to be free from self-deception. In this instance, we face the specific challenge of remembering rightly those things which, when remembered wrongly and selectively, allow for a more powerful and normative claim to being in control, of setting the terms under which everyone is to think (since it has always been this way and we have always been in charge). Put differently, Nietzsche did not intend to challenge Christian thought in this precise way, even though he sharpens the challenge: Can Christian identity claim a way of life that is continually open to correction on account of its living of a positive ethic? Can Christianity tell the truth about its past, especially its past wrongs, in a way that arises from its positive mission? Since telling the truth means admitting prior fault or wrongness, those who bear testimony about the past cannot be infallible with respect to their inheritance of that past, not only because this precludes admitting any wrong, but more importantly because Christian testimony accepts the limitations of being human because of what is *now* claimed to be true, namely that Christ is *now* Lord.

As with the possibility of forgiveness we discussed in Chapter 3, the ability to speak the truth about the past is actually *part of* the church's witness and not an impediment to it. "It is a specific element of the Christian message that there is a remedy for a bad record. If the element of repentance is not acted out in interfaith contact, we are not sharing the whole gospel witness."[43] This means that an infallible witness, perhaps ironically, cannot be a true witness because being truthful about the past always involves repentance. There is always the need truthfully to recount and thereby confess wrong regarding those things done and those things left undone. The *Übermensch* makes no confession but this does not grant him a monopoly on positive ethics. Moreover, the present confession that Christ is Lord means that past confessions of that Lordship may have, in fact, constituted denials; not now admitting fault only continues to deny Christ—even if it purports to be in the form of proclaiming him. For this reason, we may affirm that the church ought always to cultivate a readiness to reform—being a truthful people requires it.[44] Telling the truth about Jesus means not privileging the way he is remembered in a way that precludes the possibility for appealing to it and returning to it more faithfully.[45]

I contend that this is a positive ethic that includes *within it* an obligation to be honest about the past. This is the case even and especially when the truth about the past is not easily known since what is primary is not discourse about the past but a *determination*— a will—to be truthful about it even when it is painful. We can acknowledge that the affinities with Nietzsche are not finally in the particulars but in the spirit of a strong identity that does not realize its own strength through overpowering others (since this too may only be a sign of the resentment of the strong) and a refusal to repose in the comfort brought by a selective rendering of one's own past.

Chapter 6

Dispelling being

Even though Nietzsche is the great destroyer of idols, he does not rejoice that God is dead. His apocalyptic herald, Zarathustra, cowers at the thought and is nearly overwhelmed by the consequences.[1] His rapturous gospel is also partly lament:

> But how have we done this? How were we able to drink up the sea? Who gave us the sponge to wipe away the entire horizon? What did we do when we unchained this earth from its sun? Whither is it moving now? Away from all suns? Are we not plunging continually? Backward, sideward, forward, in all directions? Is there any up or down left? Are we not straying as through an infinite nothing? Do we not feel the breath of empty space? Has it not become colder?[2]

This terrible event leaves the madman (and Zarathustra) with seemingly endless questions of this sort. They are all questions that hint at nihilism, the situation that sets in when the God of morality is gone. The sun is both the anchor to earth's constancy and the astral life-giver but it is the former that is potentially catastrophic and calls forth with urgency the refrain: be faithful to the earth. Nietzsche surely thought that the death of the God of morality is more monumental than the death of the God of metaphysics since, in his genealogy, the only reason the latter ever existed in the first place was to serve the function of the former.[3]

Nevertheless, Nietzsche's mind was occupied with many things including the ways that philosophy, especially since Plato, has been obsessed with metaphysics. Christianity, as we have seen, was no different from Platonism in Nietzsche's estimation. Both not only posit two worlds (the apparent and the hidden world behind it) but also attach valuations to them, ranking the hidden world more important, a move Nietzsche only sees as inimical to human life. "The true world—unattainable, indemonstrable, unpromisable; but the very thought of it—a consolation, an obligation, an imperative."[4] Against this, human minds ought to restrict the horizon of their conjectures to those things they can conceive. As infinite, God is beyond that horizon, beyond human comprehension; in making this discovery through reason, the former consolation is lost, as is the morality it engendered. After all, Nietzsche asks, "how could something unknown obligate us?"[5] The Platonic "true world" is then not only reduced to an incredulous postulate through reason but it now fails to perform a positive function, something the *Übermensch* and other free spirits will welcome as they do the break of day, a glorious new possibility served over breakfast with unhesitating resolve to end the reign of the "true world": "let us abolish it!"[6] This is not an inevitable process but one that calls for creative wills. Yet in some ways, the process is also a natural consequence of a maturing reason: the finite mind attempts to grasp the infinite and, failing to do so, subsequently both disparages the finite for its failure even while it tries to hold onto God's infinity as a possibility.

We must permit ourselves no facile rebuttal even while Christian theology too has generally affirmed the unattainability of the infinite; yet it has not concluded that God is not worth discussing. Instead, it chastens the zeal in its own speech about God. It admits the incompatibility of human thought and speech to God's infinite being and all his other attributes. One way that Christianity chastens God-talk is through the mystery named by the Trinity. This is, therefore, a case where Nietzsche's willingness to smash idols is welcome to Christian theology.

Inasmuch as "God" can name something nonspecific or at least make reference to God without referring to Jesus Christ, the danger of idolatry is present. It refers to a generic entity that becomes quite conceivable apart from biblical revelation and Christian witness. So long as god names a kind of genus that can be known apart from the species the God of Abraham and Jesus Christ is, then the latter cannot be unique, meaning that Christians and Jews cannot truly be monotheists; they must either be polytheists who know the concept of god before "the God of our Fathers" introduces himself to Abram in Ur of the Chaldeans, to Moses in the blazing foliage of the wilderness, and to Mary in her son or else they must be idolaters of the most subtle sort, accounting preeminence to a human image of the divine (which is always ever still a human image). This is the reason that Karl Barth refused theological prolegomena and why, in the main, the Christian tradition has not advanced "God" as a word for the divine *ousia* (in Greek thought) or, indeed, a word that refers to any form (in Scholastic thought).[7] Defining terms ahead of time, like marking out the boundaries of the subsequent discourse theology names, cannot help but constrain God's revelation to *a priori* categories.

Nietzsche assails the "true world" on these precise grounds. Such a world only persists and only functions usefully as long as it can be known with some assurances, at least at the level of being able to exert itself in the obligations that transfer moral codes (highest meanings, noble purposes) to the otherwise feckless pursuits of human striving. This, in short, is how "God" functions. And it is easy to appreciate how "God," so functioning, is, in the more explicitly religious domains, construed as a metaphysical category within which different names are substituted. It is not difficult to assume that everyone knows what a god is and the only question to be decided is that of his specific identity. A variant assumption is that "religion" names a class within which different but categorically equivalent religions are arranged, an assumption that has been shown cannot withstand very much scrutiny.[8] The categories notoriously break down; the concepts believed to be shared by all religions turn out to be more complicated. Some forms of Buddhism, for example, have no concept of God. Why is Platonism a philosophy and not a religion? How is it that capitalism seems to hold the souls of its adherents and exact a kind of religious conformity but it escapes being categorized among the religions?

Yet it is not possible for "God" to function as a category in this way without establishing other gods on the same horizon exactly insofar as they submit to the same categorical schema. This is why Nietzsche called God an idol. We may likewise surmise that where God is the "higher power" of self-help groups, the concept "power" admits to gradations—of higher and lower manifestations—but as such names a recognizable notion that, in its expressions, will only differ in respect of more or less, this kind or that kind. Likewise, calling God a "supreme being" reduces all considerations to the level of being where it is assumed that we know what it is for something to have being, even though we accept that there is one that is biggest, strongest, and characterized by all other superlatives. In both cases (power and being), the metaphysical category remains established and unwavering. To identify this as a flaw is to begin to be able to identify idols and it is a Nietzschean protest that resembles parallel grievances against epistemology and morality we have explored in earlier chapters. If he is read as primarily one who offers dressed up arguments for atheism, Nietzsche's proclamation of the coming of "new gods" will strike readers as contradictory. However, his target cannot be god-as-such since this is a category he refuses to accept. It is a refusal Christian thought must share even when it cannot follow Nietzsche through to his final conclusions.

As with other aspects in Nietzsche's thought, here too the attempt to do without metaphysics is actually fraught with its own metaphysical assertions. The "new gods" are assertions of the will to power—itself a metaphysical concept even if it is not other-worldly—since to perceive them, the supreme category of being (will to power) must be accepted as the sphere within which they will be perceived. Jean-Luc Marion thus concludes that Nietzsche has not smashed *all* idols, but just the idols of the moral God. What Nietzsche erects in its place is just an idol in another guise since it too submits to a metaphysical account of being.[9] Saying this of Nietzsche differs from either claiming that his account of the Christian God is flawed or that he was mistaken to abolish the notion of god-as-otherworldly. This observation actually shares a considerable agenda with Nietzsche himself; it is closer to home for Nietzsche's own aspirations since it points out an inconsistency: the great smasher of idols has only made room for more idols after all.

Here a paradox, partially seen earlier, comes into view. While the question "What kind of being is God?" has usually been quite meaningless to Christian theology (and certainly foreign to biblical thinking), it crucially differs from the question "Does God have being?" The latter issues in answers that trade in analogy where the Being of beings does not lie along the same horizon as God's Being. We may mostly set aside the monumental literature produced in recent years in connection with Heidegger just as we need not rehearse the way that being came to denote a univocal rather than analogical concept in late medieval formulations to see how this movement registers a corruption. Nietzsche targeted the moral God for being the highest aspiration of a people who are consumed by resentment; and while he left the metaphysical God relatively untouched, his critique may be extended in service to theology.

"God" is the same thing to both theism and atheism even while one affirms its being and the other denies it. What they have in common, though, are their claims to be able to grasp what it would be for this God to be, to exist. Their relative affirmations and denials are of known quantities, not of God's personality, but of his existence. But a God whose transcendent existence is apprehended in these ways (again, affirming or denying such existence is beside the metaphysical point) cannot truly be transcendent, but must only represent the highest—*while still finite*—aspirations of a people. "Transcendent" loses its value as a true descriptor, employed instead in a manner that means something more akin to "very big" or "very high." As a philosophical concept, it has all the limitations of concepts and certainly cannot be very divine, as Heidegger explains: "Man can neither pray nor sacrifice to this God. Before the *causa sui*, man can neither fall to his knees in awe nor can he play music and dance before this god."[10] When granted existence, the god of metaphysics will not do anything divine, but will always be limited to what *metaphysics* does—this is not really a "god of metaphysics" at all, but in reality, this god is nothing other than metaphysics itself: "Metaphysics" with nothing beside or outside it, a concept to be wielded philosophically and, like all arguments and concepts, accepted or denied, but never free and never truly transcendent. The god of metaphysics is easily killed. Nietzsche's advocacy of "new gods" may be taken for its refusal to acquiesce to the regnant accounts even while any gods he would propose cannot help being subject to the iconoclasm of subsequent Nietzschean enthusiasts.

On the other hand, the worship of God as Trinity, however full of mystery, does say something about God's very being. Yet the being of this God is not a thing, a possession; it is an activity and—we may precisely say, heavily intoning Nietzsche—a *life* (as Jenson says, God is a "sequentially palpable event, like a kiss or a train wreck"[11]). The being of God is an activity where the identities of the Father, Son, and Holy Spirit are God in their mutuality, which is to say, mutual motion constituting the communal life (which is the only life) of God. The reason why God is not a being is therefore the same reason God is not simply "the infinite" as philosophy can understand both. It is not only that the *idea* of God does not submit to a more general formulation but that a category mistake has occurred when "idea" restrains (by supervening on) the act of being that God is. Put differently, the Christian God cannot be the God of metaphysics since the being of God is a Trinitarian life.

What makes idolatry pernicious and subject to the ridicule of the biblical prophets is that the idols are made of inert materials and are in the form of creatures. They cannot walk, but need to be carried; they sit like scarecrows and cannot speak, as Jeremiah's prophecy says.[12] They are carved from wood or stone, fashioned from gold or silver. Nietzsche cannot have objected to these aspects of idolatry, though. Various species of the earth itself made into idols might actually be preferable to the Christian God for one such as Nietzsche. They are reminders to be faithful to the earth and need not call to mind anything otherworldly. But in practice they do; and it is this use of the earth in drawing attention away from the earth that Nietzsche abhors. This corresponds to the biblical prophets' straightforward claim that the gods of these idols simply do not exist. Nietzsche might say, "of course they don't, but why can the idols not still be gods?"

The Dionysian view of life attests to and celebrates the excessiveness of things. In Rowan Williams's phrase (following Jacques Maritain), "things are more than what they are."[13] Reality is not exhausted by surfaces but enables the artistic display of depths. And without reducing the cosmological inheritance of the Christian West to naturalism, Nietzsche still sought accounts in which transcendence was expunged. But if the Dionysian makes its own metaphysical claims or even itself names a determinate metaphysics (as I think it does) then its overflow, its overabundance, its excessiveness, its "more" returns the indeterminacy of contingency to life. Reality, then, is at odds with every idol, every Apollonian sculpture that erects itself as an infallible—because exhaustive—mirror. In Marion's insightful analysis of the idol and the icon, the idol "places its center of gravity in a human gaze."[14] The object of the gaze is the finite reality of the idol such that the divine reality is rendered wholly visible to the intention of the gaze and therefore the gaze remains within complete possession of the idol.

In contrast, Marion adduces, the icon draws the gaze beyond itself, beyond the visible image of the invisible infinite reality. The human gaze falls on the icon only to be refocused again and again. The intention of the gaze is not permitted to remain frozen on the icon itself; it continually renounces the temptation to comprehend its true object insofar as incomprehensibility is a quality of the object's infinity (or, we must surely say, infinity *qua* infinity). To say "infinity" here, of course, is simply to say "God" since only God is infinite; but saying God then cannot be to voice a knowledge, a "meaning" that passes to a finite thing that is in any way absolute, fixed, or static. Such knowledge belongs only to the idol not the icon. The idol witnesses to a way of knowing that accepts the meaning of infinity through extrapolation and expansion of its already available concepts of finitude; while this admits to a sort of disjunction between the finite and the infinite, it only *appears* to do so while in fact sustaining their common categorization on the same plane or, as notoriously in the thought of Duns Scotus, a "chain of being" that even includes nonbeing. To say "infinity" here may also merely beg the serious question: infinite *what*? But this only illuminates the aporias that attend to this kind of discourse. We are perhaps tempted to say "infinite *being*" or "infinite *existence*" but these still suffer from the same problem as does infinity-as-such since, in all cases, we can only stretch those categories which we know in their finitude.

I shall return to the difference this makes to Christian metaphysics below. We may, however, register a determination: that Christian thought must surely welcome Nietzsche's assistance in sounding out every idol. And when he sounds out the Christian God who turns out also to be an idol, Christianity must not too quickly dismiss him, but must repent of its idolatry. Where God's being is reduced to any comprehensible "meaning," the Christian icons have failed to reflect in the human gaze the glory of God, as

Saint Paul says: "And we all, with unveiled face, beholding the glory of the Lord, are being changed into his likeness from one degree of glory to another; for this comes from the Lord who is the Spirit."[15]

While icons of the earth, of earthly materials, may exhaustively fill the gaze of the worshipper and satisfy Zarathustra's longing to be faithful to the earth, we may wonder what such an earth actually is. Except only when seen from the perspective of the most unimaginative and simplistic theologies, Christianity does not set God's reality over against the earth as "another world," an infinity that opposes itself to the finitude of creation. Instead, creation participates in the very being of God so long as it exists, its existence being an analogical sharing in the life of the Trinity. This neither makes creation eternal and therefore divine, nor does it detach sensible life from the "beyond" through correspondence to ideals and platonic forms. The contingencies of creation are not obliterated, subsumed in a metaphysical totality; they are preserved and animated by Trinitarian dynamism, the life of God's abundant motion. The harmony of the spheres that the stars sing is anything but a wall of sound, the constant and unchanging noise of every note eternally recurring and so, in every instant, present to the senses at once, a chaotic reverberation with only the semblance of variety and texture but in reality only the white noise of the void. The heavens declare sweet melodies of complexity but not chaos. While complexity implies order, it need not discover order in simple hierarchy or uniformity. The icon witnesses to the incomprehensible, insensible God and, by extension, the order of things even while the transformation it enacts in the face of the one who gazes on it prevents God's ordering of the cosmos from becoming a possession that may be grasped apart from participation in that which is both seen and unseen, that is, (and here, admittedly, the language must border on the ridiculous) seen the more it is unseen as it is seen in its unseenness such that what is seen is seen increasingly for what it fails to represent in view of the change this seeing performs. The order of things is not resident in things themselves, not in their correspondence to the illimitable "beyond," but precisely in the present, active participation of creation in the life of God as the dynamic relations and persons of Father, Son, and Holy Spirit.

This is the nature of the metaphysical unity Christian thought confesses in its doctrine of creation. It is important to see that Nietzsche was right to impugn metaphysical totalities for doing precisely what he says, diverting faithfulness from the earth. But he misidentified the true nature of Christian metaphysics in which the unseenness of God renews the ways that we see those things easily seen, the sensible world. Nevertheless, if the dominant Western metaphysics is *empirically* platonic-Christian, then it is a form of idealism that in Nietzsche's day would have found a more recent representative in Hegel (albeit with some very great differences). "Every page of my writings reveals my contempt for idealism."[16] Taken together, these represent various kinds of order for structuring space and time, of making sense of history by adducing progress toward a goal, of divining a greater structure that unites the whole and that is more fundamental (and original and final) than the disorder and imperfection characteristic of the sensible world along with time's perceptible scope and reach. Truth is more fundamental than any single representative true thing, completely existing in the ultimate beyond, unaffected by conative striving, free from the dialectical will to distinguish it from falsehood. Even though we will make use of these kinds of dialectical determinations to evaluate sensible things for their truth (as a jury does with respect to the testimonies it hears), truth does not finally reside in sensible things except only in part and by trace. Goodness does not just describe things that more or less resemble one another in a single respect, but exists as the ideal form of goodness simply as such. No real thing present to us can be fully good nor fully true since these qualities belong to ideals that, famously for neoplatonic thought at least, are compromised by material existence and the contingencies that supervene on them in that state.

Against all of this, we have seen that Nietzsche rejects this metaphysical tradition, though in its place, he surely posits another. Nietzsche's is a metaphysics of flux, absolute flow, constantly churning deep waters of chaos, a Heraclitean fundamental disunity at the heart of things. Thus some claim that Nietzsche is the progenitor of postmodern philosophy with his suspicion of totalizing grand theories of existence, his exaltation of disharmony and difference, and his unseating of modernity's hegemony of rationality, reasserting the Dionysian after the collapse of the Apollonian—indeed hastening that collapse. Yet the absence of totality does not equate to the absence of metaphysics; it is merely the abandonment of a tradition of metaphysical totality. We have wondered in earlier chapters whether a vision of fundamental chaos, indeterminacy, and disorder is no less totalizing than that which it opposes.

Even so, in Nietzsche's wake, postmodernity has embraced an ethic commensurate with this vision. Themes of otherness and difference, now commonplaces in some realms of discourse, are those realities that elicit ethics of tolerance and respect, of refusing the temptation to bring what is different within the heavy-handed reach of the same through coercion, institutional conformity, or some other violence. The power exerted against difference is subtle and pervasive, as Foucault's exacting works show, subjecting excluded and fragile entities (like human bodies) to totalizing discipline and management. Foucault, like Nietzsche, is an anti-metaphysician, requiring him to abjure a metaphysics of power in favor of investigating concrete historical instances of power's exercise. That power takes many different forms that cannot all be comprehended prior to each encounter with it attests to its resistance to being described as a totality. Yet the processes of control turn out to be ubiquitous and a culture's truth is nothing other than its exercise of power in particular ways, suggesting that, in fact, power and violence are the ultimate reality of things.

In a thesis as poignant as it is notoriously sweeping, John Milbank suggests that all of postmodernism yields but "a single nihilistic philosophy" in which difference is rendered as a form of violence that exists at the ontological level.[17] As a metaphysics of violence, postmodern difference affirms the reality of flux as we have observed in Nietzsche, but does so in the name of an ultimate surging chaos that threatens existence with its forces of pandemonium that cannot be stilled except only in appearance by Apollonian scaffolding. But then how might an alternative function? Can faithfulness to the earth in all of its particulars, then, arise from any metaphysics other than Nietzsche's (setting aside whether, in actual fact, Nietzsche's metaphysics really does make people faithful to the earth)? Can there be genuine knowledge of particulars that does not take all that exists ultimately to be subject to randomness? If Nietzsche's conflation of Christian and Platonic metaphysics is mistaken, in other words, can there be a Christian virtue of faithfulness to the earth and to the contingency of all created things that owes to its abnegation of Platonic metaphysical totality?

This is admittedly a narrow way to walk and certainly too narrow for Nietzsche whose thoughts often only came to him during walks lasting six to eight hours—through city centers or high mountain peaks. If the Christian metaphysics just explicated suggests that "flux" need not *always* name chaotic motion, then it is on these grounds that Milbank thinks the two accounts may still relate with some benefit:

> Christianity can become "internally" postmodern . . .
> I mean by this that it is possible to construe Christianity as suspicious of notions of fixed "essences" in its approach to human beings, to nature, to community and to God, even if it has never fully escaped the grasp of a "totalizing" metaphysics. Through its belief in creation from nothing it admits temporality, the priority of becoming and unexpected emergence. A reality suspended between nothing and infinity is a reality of flux, a reality without substance, composed only of relational differences and ceaseless alterations. (Augustine, *De Musica*) Like nihilism, Christianity can, should, embrace the differential flux.[18]

Nevertheless, how should the flux be embraced? If the death of God releases flux to an infinite number of chance encounters always threatening violence through its account of difference then, on the contrary, Christian thought posits peace rather than violence through the affirmation of original harmonious difference in the life of God. The Trinity is an eternal, mutual enactment of giving and receiving between the Father and the Son in the Holy Spirit in reciprocal relations. These exchanges of love admit to no lack in God or fundamental need of creation, making all that exists a function of overabundance and grace, which is to say that creation exists by gift rather than necessity and hence it is inherently a reality of flux. There may be a tension between Milbank's exhortation for Christianity to embrace the flux and his rejection of postmodern difference as violent except inasmuch as, while Nietzsche and others are helpful reminders of what Christian thought has known all along, they must still ultimately be discarded.

However, if Nietzsche's metaphysics is nearly unredeemable to some, its positive possibilities are being developed and extended by others who ask whether Nietzsche's politics really yields unbridled agonism or whether it in fact relies on nothing more solid than consent.[19] This question obviously follows from the attempt to negotiate the political landscape given the decline of metaphysics in the West, particularly where notions of the good were formerly (at least explicitly) tied to theological goods and where the rights of rulers to govern were located within theological accounts of sovereignty and the hierarchical ordering of creation and human society. The religious worldview was not at once abandoned, only to be replaced by a *nihil* in philosophy and an anarchistic politics. Its withdrawal was more subtly brokered than this since the Enlightenment set reason in the discredited religious seat, a move Nietzsche and others see as still a religious one so long as it intends to call forth convictions that carry religious weight. This is why Zarathustra's announcement that God is dead is met with disbelief though God has actually been dead for some time. The quasi-religious exaltation of human reason, as Zarathustra might say, only masked the smell of decay.[20] In this way, Nietzsche's pronouncements are more immediately political than religious commentary.

It is also a question that entails no small amount of angst when posed in a modern situation where stakes may be dangerously high. With the decline of metaphysics, all metaphysical questions are shifted into a political register. The angst that ensues when metaphysical truth loses credibility must derive from the perceived or real loss of power for mounting a convincing argument for particular truths using formal truth-language. The Enlightenment hope that reason alone is sufficient to discern the common good and to secure societal agreement concerning it was dashed at a time when new disciplines like anthropology made plain what had actually been the case all along: such agreement really ever had more to do with power and the ascendancy of one kind of thinking over the others than it did with actual consensus.

The consensus that democracy strives for, then, was sullied by quite undemocratic ways of achieving it.

It may be possible to object that through all of this, though, nothing has ever prevented the particulars of the various traditions from still being true, from being asserted by those who hold them, or from informing and giving rise to communities that depend on these convictions as true convictions. But, as a chief outcome of all postmodern political reflection, power and truth are more intimately related than this (indeed, the crucial question has become whether truth is in fact power and nothing else). And so what has changed is something that is easy to state philosophically but difficult to maintain politically: the ability to abide by the truth of these convictions can no longer count on the aid of political force especially understood as the compelling nature of rational argument among those who make differing assertions about how to live while still finding it necessary to live together in some fashion, the force of such arguments being no less violent for ostensibly being waged on the plane of reason. This, it must be said, can in fact prove impossible to surmount for those who attempt it, especially as the ability to affirm some things as true is assailed from all sides.[21] As with so many other things, Nietzsche's politics at once attempts to expose the real source of the angst while enabling the emergence of a new kind of discourse that refuses to be overcome by it. In this respect, the strength of the one Nietzsche heralds for the future, undaunted by the danger of an outlook shaped in part by the anxieties of a people who cannot face uncertainty, is a consummately *political* strength.

We may be forgiven, however, for failing to see this at first—mistaking Nietzsche, as Mann did, for being apolitical—since politicians of this sort are simply so far removed from our experience; Nietzsche's concept must surely be a non-reality. But as I argued in Chapter 5, this Nietzschean politics is not primarily found in the state, which is why Nietzsche can actually be *anti-political* with respect to the political canons of national identity and modern liberalism. As before, here, it seems to me, a Christian non-statist politics converges with Nietzsche's. The ability to recognize that true politics does not reside in the state is a prerequisite for genuine political agency at the level of communities and traditions that inhabit the particulars of life at once irreducibly connected to local factors of time and place and in blithe indifference to the official machinations of the bureaucratic apparatus. The flux is not stilled by official power. Still, if everything is in flux and nothing is solid, how can we walk? One response to this political question is given by the political theorist William Connolly who draws on Zarathustra's account of "winter doctrines" in which the surging summertime rivers now frozen over give comfort through the illusion of being ice all the way to the bottom.[22] The illusion is accepted especially by those who are suffering, seeking relief from the enigma of affliction, desperate for an answer to the anguished question "Why?" The available answers are just as frozen as the assumption that any suitable answer must be coolly inert to be true (and where truth and suitability are indistinguishable).

It is not just truth that becomes wintery, Connolly says, but just so with other concepts like nature, divinity, identity, and ethics. And perhaps even more so, the categories themselves suggest final states with rigid boundaries. As winter doctrines, categories like "identity" have their own identities that render simplistic accounts of those things that they contain even while part of the modern predicament is the relentless inability to contain them. The definitions that condition political participation, for example, cannot help but be exclusionary, invoked as gatekeepers to a selective discourse in which decisions and deliberations are not as open to free exchange and the involvement of difference as they present themselves to be. Foucault's many analyses of modern discourses and the modes of power with which they are systematically (though still often micropolitically) excluded are thoroughly Nietzschean in their inspiration.

Identity in particular, it turns out, is relationally constituted, especially through its interactions with difference. This is not to say that one's identity is exclusively granted through its opponents, but the agonistic character of contingent social relations is a constant element in the ongoing negotiation of what it means for a people to be a people. Such negotiations by necessity extend through time since timefulness does not just clarify identity, but is part of what makes something one thing and not another *now*, even though tomorrow these claims may be made quite differently. Much can be said about political identity even though Nietzsche himself did not make of it a primary concern. Still, the complexity of the world does not disappear with the methods people find to render it intelligible since part of the complexity lies in all peoples' identities as constituted by factors that are not only beyond their control, but will always be more and less intelligible as time goes on and as one people's relations with another people are negotiated in space. If identities are not fixed, but are instead contingent and persist with ambiguous boundaries, ought we to be more or less sanguine about our political prospects?

However this question gets answered, it will be evident that it cannot be done with any satisfaction at the level of theory, suggesting that democracy is a practice before it is a philosophy. But this is only to confirm Nietzsche's more general comportment with respect to life and philosophy: philosophy as a way of life or at the least where life is anterior to philosophy. Still, Nietzsche himself disapproved of democracy and for at least two reasons. First, he thought that it issues from the culture of the last man because it wills an equality at odds with those things that are empirically evident. "The coarser organ sees much apparent equality."[23] As an ideal, equality smoothes over obvious disparities and natural differences such as the ability to rule, at which some clearly excel over others. It therefore subsumes a multitude of contingent factors of human existence under a totality at odds with its stated aims. Second, democracy may surely even disguise established forms of state power through its constant invocation in public discourse where it is granted mythic significance among those who thereby unwittingly sanction anti-democratic institutions.[24] This follows from his general suspicion of the modern state which even in democratic clothing cannot resist being an idol. But even though Nietzsche himself was antipathetic to democracy—and Foucault (for Nietzschean reasons) was merely ambivalent toward it—Connolly thinks both underestimated the extent to which a recovered, admittedly more radical account of democracy is not only compatible with their philosophies, but in some sense is called forth by them.

Democracy on this conception (what Sheldon Wolin calls "fugitive democracy") is eminently democratic as it does not speculate over political doctrines that precede political instantiation but instead recognizes the irreducible contingency, temporality, and shifting ("discordant") identity of the political actors. And if such identity is formed in relational difference, any subsequent discourse will occur separate from truth since, by definition, difference will always involve disagreement over what is true. Modern politics is predicated precisely on a situation in which political bodies are not expected to ask or answer questions about truth and may only ask about the good insofar as the latter questions are *a posteriori* descriptions of pragmatic debates and consensus-making that have already occurred. "Consensus," in other words, is the only good. What then of truth?

The connection between politics and truth is attended by two seemingly straightforward subsidiary considerations: pluralism and relativism. First is the empirical reality of pluralism in which different groups make rival claims within and outside of political discourse. But it has long been noted that pluralism does not just name political rivalry; instead, it names a situation in which any resolutions that might otherwise have been accomplished through appeals to a uniting political vision are no longer possible. Truth has not exactly dropped out of consideration as a metaphysical notion, though different groups will have varying notions of it at the level of theory (which will still be metaphysical in varying degrees) and at the level of the particulars: how the people with one political identity over another conceive of the nature of public space, whether they admit to this space as secular, how they contribute to the nature of public involvement, the pursuit of the good, and so on.

Connolly describes a typical democratic conversation that presumes the reality of pluralism. It transpires in the following way. The reality of differing notions of the social and human good is named by pluralism, evoking the question, "How can a politics of discordance validate itself?"[25] The response, then, is simply that it cannot and so it must therefore be excluded as a possibility. Such a politics cannot defend itself as a social and human good in the face of pluralism's eschewal of such doctrines. But Connolly thinks that this places too much confidence in the knowing enterprise, recalling for us the argument of Chapter 2 in which I showed how Nietzsche detects the preoccupation of modern epistemology with a two-stage approach in which the inability to prove that something ought to count as knowledge is taken to be sufficient warrant for not counting it as knowledge. Here Connolly now helps to clarify how Nietzsche's critique of modern epistemology may be given political expression (even if, as we have said before, it turns out to be an expression he himself would not have chosen). The "typical conversation" in which pluralism appears to emasculate itself as a social or political philosophy can only be fatal against the background of modern epistemology which is itself a winter doctrine. The reality of flux, only disguised in the winter frost, will not insist that pluralism substantiate itself on *a priori* grounds since the democratic exercise of deliberation, dispute, and consensus-making admits to no more fundamental reality beneath it, no notion of the common good that is not itself a shifting notion as "in flux" as the people to whom it belongs.

The second subsidiary consideration, relativism, is not an empirical reality but a philosophical doctrine that may follow from the reality of pluralism. In relativism, truth has, in fact, dropped out. It cannot be said to have been refuted; only that it has failed to sustain sufficient interest politically and possibly otherwise. At earlier points in this book, we were driven to ask whether Nietzsche, who clearly acknowledges the reality of pluralism, is a relativist with regard to truth. The problem, though, is not just that this enlists him in an analytical debate foreign to him, but that the tendency to read his perspectivism this way obscures the highly ethical dimension of his thought, threatening to turn him into a representative of the nihilism he opposes. Particularly insofar as relativism is a philosophical doctrine, it is always in the position of overdetermining the political exercise of actual pluralistic communities. And the same must surely be said of secularism as long as it too suggests a theory one can advocate rather than a reality one can name.

Connolly frequently makes reference to the disparity Nietzsche helps to identify between the ideals of social constitution and actual social existence. He takes Nietzsche to be instructive for identifying a third way among communitarians and individualist-liberals.[26] It becomes relatively straightforward to identify that both sides of this binary choice eschew the ambiguities of social life and its discordant elements once the political sphere is described in a Nietzschean fashion. Communitarians seek a unity that is not actually there while individualist-liberals refuse to seek such unity in an attempt to avoid totalitarianism. The former is preoccupied with elaborating the good and the latter with enumerating and securing rights. But neither premises political discourse on difference within the body politic (itself a shifting body) as a positive contribution. Whether or not truth has actually dropped out of political consideration is an empirical question to be answered through observation rather than a philosophical question to be answered through theory. The analogous *political* question that occupied Nietzsche was not concerned with truth but with the will to truth, a will that a people will invariably display, often despite themselves. What is the will to truth?

As I showed in Chapter 2, Nietzsche's rejection of truth was, in one respect, only a rejection of the correspondence theory of truth. These theories are controlling concepts that only find truth where the theory permits and, as such, fall victim to Nietzsche's critiques of metaphysics. Christian thought, I argued, likewise positions the knower of truth within the very substance of the truth through participation, through a present constitution that affords knowledge of the truth only insofar as it is the truth that constitutes the life of the knower. In this respect, truth is not a static entity about which information may be dispensed, served by distance, and upheld by the logic of separation—knower from known. Instead, the dynamics of truth are revealed by modes that are less straightforwardly dispensations: narrative (especially tragedy) and aphorism in which some ways of life make some knowers better attuned to truth than others. This, I argued, is why theological arguments that attempt to prove the existence of truth based on logical arguments alone suffer from an impoverished account both of truth and of knowledge.

Near the end of his sane life, Nietzsche's fascination with the will to power itself increasingly became a fascination with a metaphysical concept. Did he fall into contradiction with what he earlier said about truth and knowledge? When claiming that life is the will to power *and nothing else*, he is clearly drawn to the grandness of all-encompassing explanations of the very sort he also wants to reject. But if the will to power is a metaphysical concept, it is not metaphysical in the same respect as those that he rejects. In their least salutary modes, metaphysical concepts are unitary, reducing everything to a single thing. Will to power does this, even though "will" is not itself simple: it is an activity rather than a state, exercised rather than experienced, temporal and spatial like life itself. Furthermore, the complexity of the will to power is found in the many ways that the will is expressed, and it never exists *as such*, but only in this or that instance where it is identified by the process it enacts over against the obstacles that resist it. Put differently, the will to power never shows itself as will to power, only as a second-order willing that stands behind other activities (which is why Foucault, despite his tendency to find power everywhere, insists that power is only recognized in discursive practices: torture and punishment, mental illness, human sexuality, and so on).

It is only against this background that we can understand what Nietzsche means by the will to truth. Nietzsche recognized that the desire for the truth is a strong desire and one that is not easily subjugated (knowingly, at least) to other wills, other desires. It is certainly the case that we would often rather believe fictions and take pleasure in the comforts they afford, but we will not willfully lie to ourselves about our belief in fictions, which is to say, even our belief in fictions submits to our will to truth inasmuch as we believe fictions precisely because we believe them to be true. Hence, the will to truth triumphs even though not everything we believe and know is true. Nietzsche was troubled by how his anti-metaphysical sensibilities seemingly were insufficient to overcome the will to truth.[27] Truth more easily bends before critique than does the will to truth. After all, what is it that gives shape to any critique if not the desire to find the truth about the thing critiqued? But then this is still a form of Christianity, a will that is still shaped—despite everything else—by moral notions that, Nietzsche feared, were at some level even metaphysical.

[Y]ou will have gathered what I am getting at, namely, that it is still a *metaphysical faith* upon which our faith in science rests—that even we knowers of today, we godless anti-metaphysicians, still take *our* fire, too, from the flame lit by the thousand-year-old faith, the Christian faith which was also Plato's faith, that God is truth; that truth is divine.[28]

The will to truth, then, wills itself. It is the desire that even-tuates in its own discovery; it cannot be exercised and denied at the same time and there is no way even to begin to deny it apart from setting out by way of exercising it. To discover the truth about the will to truth will certainly require the will to truth. It becomes metaphysical precisely at this point: the will to truth, like all metaphysical concepts, seems to undervalue all pursuits by positing an end in mind that is knowable apart from attaining it, reachable without pursuit. Is the will to truth really *knowable* without the *exercise* of the will to truth? Or is the problem merely that it *is* always known by it? Either way, there is a problem. In the first case, the problem is that the will to truth seems to contradict the will to power and enervate life; in the second case, it is that the pursuits of ascetics—through subjecting their lives to severity and rejecting spontaneity—seem actually to be justified.

Nietzsche claims that the problem he identifies is nothing other than the will to truth becoming conscious of itself. This, he says, is the final stage in Christianity's self-destruction. Christian morality will suffer its own mortal blow when it asks itself, "What does all will to truth mean?"[29] And he offers an answer:

> [W]hat meaning does *our* being have, if it were not that
> the will to truth has become conscious of itself *as a problem*
> in us? . . . Without a doubt, from now on, morality will be
> *destroyed* by the will to truth's becoming-conscious-of-itself:
> that great drama in a hundred acts reserved for Europe in
> the next two centuries, the most terrible, the most dubious
> drama but perhaps also the one most rich in hope . . .[30]

In other words, human meaning is bound up with the recent loss of meaning that resulted when the will to truth was exposed as a *will* by those who turned from their pursuit of truth to look at it. For Nietzsche, this is a contradiction with potentially nihilistic consequences, hence his prognostications for the future of Europe. But as we have seen before, nihilism is not the only option. The future may also be "the one most rich in hope" because it lies open for those who would rescue life from being hated, as is enshrined in Christian morality and, by extension, metaphysical explanations of meaning. Rather than assuming that the will to truth is proved by the tautology he noted above, he instead assumes that it is exposed as unfounded. He continues to make every attempt to be a consistent anti-metaphysician.

However, let us press Nietzsche further on this point. If the will to truth is a meaning-producing desire, sanctioned by a covert human hatred of the body and the senses—death and decay, suffering and unrequited yearning—then it is fundamentally, as he claims, a hatred of life. Even so, it is still an exemplification of the will to power. The overcoming of obstacles that Christianity seeks, including the falsehood named by the will to truth, is a desire for power over the limitations, transience, and meaninglessness of life. Asceticism may appear to reject power through the discipline of the body, but even this is just a disguise, its will to power appearing as humility that secretly wills to reverse the ascendancy of the proud. The will to truth cannot have metaphysical status but the will to power may.[31]

Yet (this finally being the crucial point), Nietzsche loves life—and with no hint of sentimentality. If Christianity found reasons for hating life, Nietzsche does not propose mere counter-reasons, but an affirmation of life after all such reasons have been heard and discredited. His is a love irrespective of straightforward justification. The more one loves life, the more one will exercise the will to power. This is because the will to power does not finally will a *thing*; power is not an object that is obtained and grasped; "power is exercised rather than possessed," as Deleuze puts it.[32] It is realized in the activity of willing it, of pursuing it. As time went on and Nietzsche increasingly equated the will to power with life itself, he did so because living life has value quite apart from its pursuit of a distant (transcendent) object; its value resides in the activity of living. True living both comes from and takes the form of the love of life or, put differently, to love life is to live it and vice versa. And if we are led to ask what it is that makes life loveable, we have already given up because such questions are only asked by those who will never find an adequate answer. "You look up," advises Zarathustra, "when you feel the need for elevation. And I look down because I am elevated."[33] Neither love nor life answer to a more fundamental criterion since any such criterion would only supply reasons for discontinuing the activities of love and life that are pursued for their own sakes; this leads ineluctably to nihilism.[34]

Consider that this really is the case with love. When the lover is asked, "Why do you love me?" surely no answer can suffice: not the beauty of the beloved nor her constancy, nor any such things that, like life itself, fade and change over time. A lover who loves for beauty is shallow, though the lover surely finds beauty in the beloved. In the same way, friendships do not exist for reasons that can be enumerated without implying that they therefore exist for convenience and out of utility. Love, friendship, and life are their own goods, desirable for their own sakes. But we must immediately qualify this by stating the obvious: something desirable for its own sake not only rebuffs *reasons* for desiring it, but crucially also knows nothing that will satisfy the desire, nothing that, once obtained, will signal the end of the desire as, on one understanding as we have already seen in Chapter 4, food is to hunger. If hunger is the desire for food and is satisfied with food, what does love desire that may similarly satisfy it? Nietzsche's insight in the will to power is that, as the exercise of the love of life, there is a desire named by love that is only satisfied in its exercise rather than in the grasping of an object since love is not oriented to a thing.

Still, love precedes even life. Zarathustra goes on, "we love life, not because we are used to living but because we are used to loving."[35] We (at least insofar as we follow Zarathustra) do not love life because we have assessed life and found it lovable but because the *will* to love precedes any turning to life exactly to the extent that life is not knowable apart from being lived just as it is not livable apart from being loved. And what about suffering? If life is suffering, as Schopenhauer believed and with which Nietzsche concurred, then suffering occupies exactly the same space (for Nietzsche) as the will to power, meaning that they cannot be at odds, as we have seen—whether meeting an obstacle causes suffering is beside the point. And if any strategy for assessing the meaning of suffering is bound to fail on account that any available vantage for doing so is already an active participation in the very life of suffering it would otherwise seek to overcome, then one must surely hate life by refusing suffering. Furthermore, not only must one hate life, but one will have sought and have found a passive orientation to life that compromises the will to power life names such that in refusing suffering, the will is denied its life-generating and life-constituting value. Life against suffering, then, is life toward death.

If its response to suffering potentially destabilizes a Christian validation to life, then it must be acknowledged that the genius of Christianity with regard to suffering is simply not what Nietzsche thinks. It is not its discovery of an unassailable theodicy, its ability to account for the fact that all suffer unjustly in one way or the other, subject to the contingencies of history but nourished on satisfying placebos of overarching grand plans and meaningful-because-heroic stories of undergoing affliction for the greater good. After all, where is this wonderfully successful theodicy? Is not the "problem" precisely that all theodicies are notoriously inadequate? The more successful the theodicy, it seems, the more it looks as if Nietzsche is vindicated: suffering is not so much muddled through and coped with, but *denied*. And, of course, where suffering is denied, life cannot be affirmed. Even so, where Christian thought, like Job's so-called friends, has taken up attempts to explain suffering, it has failed miserably. It is in the midst of the explanations of Job's suffering by Eliphaz the Temanite, Bildad the Shuhite, and Zophar the Naamathite that he declares "I loathe my life."[36] We might, with Nietzsche, surmise that such loathing is as much a function of the explanations as of the suffering, and as much a function of their success in explaining as of their failure. After all, when Job finally is addressed by the voice from the whirlwind, all of the theodicies hitherto proffered are decidedly not refuted but devastatingly shown to rely on limited knowledge; Job too finally confesses, "Therefore I have uttered what I did not understand, things too wonderful for me, which I did not know."[37] Satan's question to God at the start of the narrative had, of course, not been theoretical, but eminently practical: "Does Job fear God for naught?"[38] The question is not one that is answered by reasons or explanations, but by the will. And the answer the will gives is itself given through the exercise of the will (something impossible for theodicy, which we may carefully judge to be its precise weakness and impossibility); understanding and knowl-edge were category mistakes with respect to the practicality of the question about Job's suffering. Further still, we do well to recall that Satan's question was not actually about suffering at all, but about love, whether love is independent of suffering, whether *Job's* love of God was instrumental to even the slightest degree. An explained suffering is not adequate to suffering, but, more importantly, an explained love is inadequate to love and even positively imperils love's exercise—or, with Nietzsche, *life's* exercise.

It will already be surmised that much of this makes Nietzsche's thinking profoundly Christian. His dismissals of Christianity were not always theologically well-informed and, even though in the present book I have tried to resist arguing with him at every point, here is a place where Christian thought should notice that much of what he rejects is also rejected by a great deal of theology, even though Nietzsche probably did not know it. Nietzsche's love for life, like Job's love for God, must be "for naught." In the same way, Christian worship of God may benefit those who worship, but Christians do not worship God to receive benefit; God may bring comfort but Christians do not worship God to be comforted. The difference is that Nietzsche sought to expose through genealogy the fact that, despite everything else, Christians *actually do* worship God for instrumental reasons. Where this is the case descriptively, the appropriate response to Nietzsche is not refutation but repentance. And where it is not the case, Christian thought should seize the opportunity to clarify that it has, at its best, never counseled anything but a noninstrumental "for naught," a sharp separation (in terms that admittedly owe more to Nietzsche than biblical religion) between will and knowledge where knowledge dwells in explanations that circumvent the exercise of the will, but also an appropriate intermingling of love with life, knowledge with both seeing and not seeing.

The "beyond" in which Christian confession places God is not attainable by ascent of the mind nor the rise of the soul *from* life. Creaturely longing for God, it is true, is a longing for what is unlimited and infinite. God, beyond human knowledge and grasp, lifts the sights of creatures to himself even though God is not beheld by knowledge. Delight, then, in God's beauty is a love for God that is realized only as the continual process of following, as Gregory of Nyssa said of Moses.[39] Hidden in the cleft of the rock, Moses sees only God's backside as the ineffable God passes before him. Such seeing is one with following, more movement than static gaze. Not only does the infinite beauty of God exceed human knowledge but also the invitation to know God is precisely given as the invitation to know God *as unknowable*, ever moving forward and bidding follow. To persist in following an ungraspable God is eminently absent the consolation of any metaphysics, Christian, Platonist, or otherwise. As Gregory says, "To follow God wherever he might lead is to behold God."[40]

This is a life of motion where the motion is itself the desire for God, never satisfied by seeing God and yet not as an endless deferral of satisfaction (the beatific vision must come, but it is obviously not for us a knowledge). It is a satisfaction that is continually met and exceeded even as Nietzsche described life (here as the will to power) as only being satisfied by that which, by necessity, must also in some sense fail to satisfy, only because it pushes forward, constantly overcoming itself.[41] Longing for God is met in loving and following only to be exceeded again by a greater longing, calling forth deeper loving, and more steadfast following. As Augustine noted, unlike other things, love is not diminished when it is exercised, experienced, given away. It is not used up because its bounty will always exceed every initial assessment just as the fullness of God is beheld with a vision that sees God as more than what appears to the senses. But this is not a disparagement of the body in the ways that Nietzsche has made familiar to us. It is the very affirmation of the active life, a refusal to be granted what we ask for in completion since, with this, we would with satiated desires only then have reason to abandon life. But to see God is to want more of God, to look up is not to cease in desire, "but one must always," says Gregory, "by looking at what he can see, rekindle his desire to see more."[42]

Metaphysics is inimical to life when it forsakes faithfulness to the earth by encouraging desires that cannot be fulfilled, as it were, on earth. But even for Nietzsche, life and the earth are not first principles. Resolving to "love the earth" is a quite meaningless intention that at least threatens to make an idol out of the earth. Life is loved by those who, as Zarathustra says, are used to loving. And how shall we conceive of the love of life in light of the love of God? Those used to loving God will surely be used to having their desires enlarged by the abundant vision of a God never fully beheld even while loving and seeing are together forever exceeding each other. When love comes, as the goal sought, the seeking is not over, neither is the goal left behind. What, then, is now possible for a practiced love that does not have any less to give? As one commentator observes of Nietzsche's affirmation of life, 'Only the will to love can enable man to discover the potentially lovable sides of life . . .'[43] This is because even knowledge (what there is to be known about life) is second to the anterior desire to love life which, in turn, is surely nothing other than love itself.[44]

It must be acknowledged that the will to power is intentionally structured as activity without future hope and so is expressed as *incessant* activity. If there is an object of desire that is future, then the will to power will seek it even while in doing so, it will exhaust itself of its present activity. The Eternal Recurrence prohibits future hope of this kind to preserve the active will to power and the love of life. What is eternal is crucially not future. To Nietzsche, limitless possibilities were always only to be discovered apart from hope; the *present* is limitless precisely because it recurs eternally. This, of course, means that in a sense past, present, and future are all the same in respect of their eternality and so, as Nietzsche saw, in all other respects. This cannot be Christian since Christianity confesses a temporally finite creation (so, for example, Basil: "What has a temporal beginning must necessarily have a temporal ending"[45]). The history of everything, indeed history itself, is made possible by the non-eternality of creation; and this also becomes the precise possibility of hope as desire for a *future* object. The crucial question, though, must be whether Christian thought and practice can maintain, in a created order that admits of a temporal and finite future, an active life that is not easily deferred by limitations it accepts on the present, due to assumptions that the depths of things are only revealed in their futurity. Its ability to do so will depend on the excellence of its love for God.

If nothing else (though it certainly is) Nietzsche's will to power is a warning that Christianity is always beset by the temptation to be satisfied with its static gazes at God rather than the active life that discipleship requires in imitation of and participation in the active life of the Trinity if it is to avoid clutching at idols. Even the self-satisfied, ostensibly vindicated priority of the will to truth must not hold back the active pursuit of truth if it is to keep from becoming a frozen (and incoherent) concept. Nietzsche's willing, even eager, destruction of idols can be selectively embraced—but still *embraced*—by Christianity. It is true that in some ways we might conclude that, as thorough as he is, in the end he is still not thorough enough since even his own gods are idols. Even so, Nietzsche knew only too well something that Christianity has never readily admitted: that even God—*especially* God!—can be an idol and theology its willing accomplice.

Chapter 7
Dancing and singing

It remains to make Nietzsche dance. The physical prowess of the noble and strong who, in their judgments, exercise the confident vivacity of masters is indeed "a powerful physicality, a blossoming, rich, even effervescent good health which includes the things needed to maintain it, war, adventure, hunting, dancing, jousting and everything else that contains strong, free, happy action."[1] But Nietzsche's own body was frequently beleaguered by physical weakness and capricious agony. When in January 1889 Franz Overbeck traveled to Turin, where Nietzsche had until recently been working on his peculiar autobiography, he reported, "I see Nietzsche huddled up reading in the corner of a sofa . . . the incomparable master of expression is incapable of conveying even the delights of his merriment in anything but the most trivial expressions or by dancing and jumping about in a comical manner."[2] Weeks earlier, Nietzsche's landlady had spied on him through the keyhole and saw him dancing naked.

It is tempting to romanticize Nietzsche's descent into insanity since it seems to affirm what is most salient about his thought. Art surpasses knowledge because life is an aesthetic experience that will always exceed our thoughts about it. And this great thinker of life was constantly finding his thinking in tension with his thoughts, life breaking through on occasion to humiliate the thinking and yield a musical ecstasy. Was he, we romantically ask, finally overcome by music? Was the overcoming even, at root, religious? "I would believe only in a god who could dance. . . . Come, let us kill the spirit of gravity! . . . Now I am light, now I fly, now I see myself beneath myself, now a god dances through me."[3]

Nietzsche desperately wanted to enable a way of life in which actions are free and spontaneous, neither random nor submitted to philosophical inquiry or morality. Such a way of life is non-instrumental. This does not mean that it accomplishes nothing, but only that it is not driven by the need to accomplish. Anything it accomplishes is only an unexpected outcome, a delight for being a contingent occurrence rather than being sought outright. His chosen image for this way of life is frequently dancing. The only explanation for dancing is joy, something that hardly explains in an ordinary sense. Joy gives rise to dancing without telling us what dancing is *for*, and this is precisely the point: it is not *for* anything, even though it may have antecedent causes. Why is so-and-so dancing? Nietzsche rightly sees that we can only give non-teleological answers to this (though an exception might be the rain dance: so-and-so is dancing to make it rain). But his whole philosophy intended a "sweeping attack on all of the 'causality' of previous philosophy."[4] The most salutary actions are done for no reason; they seek no outcome; they are not governed by careful weighing of cause and effect. They are done for no reason precisely because actions that are presided over by reason can only ever be actions of reason and thus will always fail to connect with the larger side of living. Dancing is the non-rational activity *par excellence*. We dance for the same reasons we love—for no reason at all other than the sheer joy of its exercise. Its joy *is* its exercise.

Nietzsche's life displayed an extraordinary tension between his desire and his reality. His sober and moderate lifestyle was not only lonely, but very nearly ascetic. He seems to have been morally above reproach, despite claims to being the first true immoralist. With the exception of his final insane raptures, his life was far from the exuberant celebration of life through dancing and singing. His famous rift with fellow aesthete Wagner came about as the latter turned art into a cliché, the tawdry deployment of predictably flamboyant carnivals, the attempt to make music do something, to make it serve a more fundamental purpose. Nietzsche characterizes Wagner's style in instrumental terms: "the pose is the end; the drama, also the music, is always merely its means."[5] Music became, for Wagner, a means to elicit a physiological response in view of its overwhelming acoustical bedlam:

One walks into the sea, gradually loses one's secure footing, and finally surrenders oneself to the elements without reservation: one must *swim*. In older music, what one had to do in the dainty, or solemn, or fiery back and forth, quicker and slower, was something quite different, namely, to *dance*. . . . Richard Wagner wanted a different kind of movement . . . Swimming, floating—no longer walking and dancing.[6]

Wagner only wanted to elicit an effect, "*chaos* in place of rhythm," to which no discernable pattern of movement could be matched, but only flailing arbitrariness.[7] Such music shakes the listener and is called "effective!"[8] Yet to Nietzsche, this tactic only functionalizes the art by giving the appearance of style and culture to those who can recognize such things when they are expressed only at the surface. The Dionysian spirit of life suits those whose experience of life is already overfull. The spirit yields insight into such a life while Dionysian art dispenses this insight. But those whose experience of life is the opposite—impoverishment—will want something different from their art; they will want art to provide what life does not: fury and ecstasy.[9] Art thus conspires against life, negating it, enacting its revenge against what life seems powerless to afford. This is where Nietzsche came to consign both Wagner and Schopenhauer, asking "Is it the *hatred* against life or the *excess* of life which has here become creative?"[10] Goethe, he thought, was creative with the excess of life, never didactic, whereas Wagner was merely a Euripides bringing a physiological lesson.[11]

Nevertheless, knowledge frequently kept Nietzsche from dancing. It functioned like the fault that Adorno and Horkheimer were later to pin on Odysseus who had himself bound to the mast of his boat to help him resist the sirens' song, supposing that music is something to be resisted, its affirmation of life to be denied in favor of affirming instead a vital restraint against music. "Without music, life would be an error," Nietzsche wrote. "The German imagines even God singing songs."[12] Even so, Nietzsche often resembled Zarathustra, the glad prophet who, on at least one occasion, would rather pontificate—and even sing—than dance.

When he encounters dancing girls in the forest, Zarathustra at once intones at length in praise of wisdom. When his song ends, the dance was already over, the sun had set, and the girls had left the forest. Life had passed him by even in his singing. His singing had kept him from dancing because it was not finally a song about life but instead about the love of *wisdom* as the love of life. "I am well disposed toward wisdom . . . this is because she reminds me so much of life." In the song, Zarathustra tells life that she is the wisdom he is extolling and she laughs sarcastically, "And even if you are right—should *that* be said to my face?"[13] In his sadness and loneliness, Zarathustra stands in the dark and wonders to himself that he is still alive, asking, "Why? What for? By what? Whither? Where? How? Is it not folly still to be alive?"[14] In making life into a knowledge (even a "wisdom"), Zarathustra managed to escape life's compulsion toward dancing, which is to say, life's very exercise. He wonders why he is still alive since remaining alive is at odds with his forgotten will to dance. Disastrously, he had stood at a distance. Wisdom is not the same thing as life; it deliberates on life and ponders it, but ultimately sends away the dancing girls who only ever wanted Zarathustra to join in the dance. Later, Zarathustra argues with wisdom at the tombs of his youthful dreams, wondering how his dreams were never lived, how they never even broke forth into the light of day. They had invited him to dance but wisdom did not supply the appropriate tune.

> I stood ready for the best dance, when you murdered my
> ecstasy with your sounds. Only in the dance do I know
> how to tell the parable of the highest things: and now
> my highest parable remained unspoken in my limbs.
> My highest hope remained unspoken and unredeemed.
> And all the visions and consolations of my youth died![15]

Zarathustra gives up on wisdom, which he only found inimical to the dreams of his youth, and he instead discovers the unburiable will: "something that explodes rock." The will to power is life itself since to live is to will. Nietzsche's doctrine of salvation required the death of youth's dreams at the hands of wisdom to expose the disjunction between wisdom and life and the praise of the will. When Zarathustra encounters life again in "The Other Dancing Song," she (life) accuses him of not loving her as much as he claims, to which he responds by appealing to wisdom, to knowledge.

> "Yes," I answered hesitantly, "but you also know——" and
> I whispered something into her ear, right through her

tangled yellow tresses. "You *know* that, O Zarathustra? Nobody knows that." . . . But then life was dearer to me than all my wisdom ever was.[16]

It did not matter what Zarathustra whispered about what he claimed to know; life retorted with the ultimate epistemological trump, refuting the ability of anybody to know it. What Zarathustra could not countenance until that moment was that his own faithfulness to life did not depend on knowledge. Now Zarathustra could *will* to dance, no longer held back by the entombed, once youthful silences; life had shared the secret of salvation. After all, "only where there are tombs are there resurrections."[17]

Nietzsche would have believed in a god who can dance. Not only must God dance but such a singular belief must itself be dance-like more than belief-like if God is to be freed from the shackles of reason writ large. Christianity failed Nietzsche in the same way that Zarathustra disappointed life herself. An early commentator asks:

> May it not be that many of the ills from which society suffers and for which Nietzsche held Christianity in part at least responsible are due less to the fact that Christian principles and morals exist at all than to the fact that they have not been lived enough? The Christianity which Nietzsche attacks is an incomplete, hesitating, illogical movement, most of whose followers are afraid to see it through to the finish.[18]

Equally, theology surely failed Nietzsche since Christianity in fact holds that God is himself both a dance and his own music. The Father, Son, and Holy Spirit are an unending, infinitely complex harmony whose relations are pure music. The joy of divine fellowship does not exist for the benefit of creation though creation may benefit from it. The Trinitarian life is itself a non-instrumental dance of joy. Still, Nietzsche was all too human. He had the impulse to sing and generally found ways to avoid singing. But he was surely more genuinely human than most are, for whom belief in God needs no singing and no dancing. His impulse was much stronger than most. If the spirit of music gives birth to authentic human reality, then the reality of music births a deeper reality still: the human dance is existence before a God who was already dancing. The true mystery is why, among the living, singing and dancing are not more common. It is a mystery which Nietzsche discerned with extraordinary clarity.

Notes

Introduction

[1] Frederick Copleston, S. J., *Friedrich Nietzsche: Philosopher of Culture* (New York: Harper & Row, 1974), xi.

[2] We must also recognize that Nietzsche on occasion reflected more cheerfully on his attacks on Christianity.

> [T]o attack is with me a proof of good will, under certain circumstances of gratitude. . . . If I wage war on Christianity I have a right to do so, because I have never experienced anything disagreeable or frustrating from that direction—the most serious Christians have always been well disposed towards me. I myself, an opponent of Christianity *de rigueur*, am far from bearing a grudge against the individual for what is the fatality of millennia. (*EH*, "Why I am so Wise," 7)

[3] To be sure, the assumption of modern secularism that God is not present in the other disciplines is not an acceptable strategy for granting theology its distinctiveness.

[4] *A*, 62.

[5] Karl Barth, *Church Dogmatics* I/1, trans. G. W. Bromiley et al. (Edinburgh: T&T Clark, 1956–1975), 60.

[6] *Z*, Prologue, 6.

[7] That is, except for the words of worship, the primary discourse of liturgy, as Catherine Pickstock has argued in *After Writing: On the Liturgical Consummation of Philosophy* (Oxford: Blackwell, 1997).

[8] *TL*, 1.

[9] As Robert Jenson notes, theology is "the thinking internal to the task of speaking the gospel, whether to humankind as a message or to God in praise and petition." Robert W. Jenson, *Systematic Theology: The Triune God*, vol. 1 (Oxford: Oxford University Press, 1997), 5.

[10] *WP*, 481.

[11] I am aware that I am leaning here toward reading Nietzsche as a Wittgensteinian. I am not convinced that this is wrong to do. For a comparison of these two thinkers see Erich Heller, *The Importance of Nietzsche* (London: University of Chicago Press, 1988), chap. 8.

[12] As recent examples, see Tyler T. Roberts, *Contesting Spirit: Nietzsche, Affirmation, Religion* (Princeton, NJ: Princeton University Press, 1998) and Julian Young, *Nietzsche's Philosophy of Religion* (Cambridge: Cambridge University Press, 2006).

[13] Though not carelessness, as some have accused of him.

Notes

[14] *WP*, 169 cited in F. A. Lea, *The Tragic Philosopher: Friedrich Nietzsche* (London: Athlone, 1993), 339. (Lea uses a translation from the Levy edition of Nietzsche's works that preserves Nietzsche's intended caustic tone better than Kaufmann's "disastrous wrong-headed fellow"); *A*, 45.

[15] For example, most recently Stephen N. Williams, *The Shadow of the Antichrist: Nietzsche's Critique of Christianity* (Grand Rapids, MI: Baker, 2006). David Bentley Hart, *The Beauty of the Infinite: The Aesthetics of Christian Truth* (Grand Rapids, MI: Eerdmans, 2003) is in a class of its own in almost every respect.

[16] Merold Westphal, *Suspicion and Faith: The Religious Uses of Modern Atheism* (Grand Rapids, MI: Eerdmans, 1993), chap. 1.

[17] Michel Foucault, *Power/Knowledge: Selected Interviews and Other Writings, 1972–1977*, ed. Colin Gordon, trans. Colin Gordon, Leo Marshall, John Mepham, Kate Soper (New York: Pantheon Books, 1980), 53–54.

Chapter 1: A catastrophic life

[1] "Sometimes these days I see no reason to accelerate the *tragic* catastrophe of my life that began with *Ecce*" (*SL*, December 16, 1888).

[2] *SL*, June 11, 1865.

[3] Cited in Rüdiger Safranski, *Nietzsche: A Philosophical Biography*, trans. Shelley Frisch (London: Granta, 2002), 357.

[4] January 18, 1876, cited in Safranski, *Nietzsche*, 362.

[5] *TI*, 34.

[6] *SL*, December 25, 1882.

[7] *HH*, I, 489.

[8] *A*, 8, 9.

[9] *TI*, "'Reason' in Philosophy," 5. And Jacques Derrida, *Of Grammatology* (Baltimore: Johns Hopkins, 1998), 14.

Chapter 2: Un-mastering knowledge

[1] Augustine, *Soliloquies*, II, 2.2.

[2] John Duns Scotus, *Commentary on the Sentences*, I, 2.1.

[3] Karl Barth, *Church Dogmatics* IV/3.1, trans. G. W Bromiley et al. (Edinburgh: T&T Clark, 1956–1975), 441.

[4] In one of his last books, Nietzsche continues to associate Socrates with an inferior mode of knowledge evinced by his dialectical approach: "What must be proved is worth little ... One chooses dialectic only when one has no other means" (*TI*, "The Problem of Socrates," 5–6).

[5] *BT*, 12.

[6] *BT*, 7.

[7] Nietzsche also faults Euripides with the death of music and the Dionysian, which are ultimately bound up with each other.

[8] For Nietzsche, tragedy is also a preeminent art form for not exalting the individual, for example, *BT*, 10.

[9] *BT*, 10.

[10] *BT*, 17. Still, it needs to be acknowledged that Nietzsche took Christianity to be hostile to life inasmuch as Christian ethics is about "absolute standards" and

therefore "from the very first, Christianity spelled life loathing itself" (*BT*, "A Critical Backward Glance," 5). Absolutes are, of course, quantities that are known ahead of time and so Nietzsche took such a view of life to be the exact opposite of his own aesthetic proposal. It clearly escaped him that Christianity could render life aesthetically.

[11] *BT*, 18.

[12] *TI*, "Reason in Philosophy," 6.

[13] *BT*, 18.

[14] Of course, putting the question this way is slightly absurd since contingency can never be rendered necessary without ceasing to be contingent. But this only highlights the difficulty in talking in these terms since contingency seems inescapably always to presuppose some telos considering that we seem driven to ask, "contingent on *what*?" But any answer to that question makes contingency an incoherent concept.

[15] *TI*, "Reason in Philosophy," 6. See also *WP*, 1052: "the Dionysus of the Greeks: the religious affirmation of life, life whole and not denied or in part."

[16] *BT*, 9.

[17] *Ibid.*, 9.

[18] Arthur C. Danto points out as much, suggesting that Nietzsche's metaphysics of flux remained an inextirpable element in his thought that then could not help but eventuate in the notion of the will to power which, for Danto, is nothing if not metaphysical and therefore self-contradictorily nihilistic.

> In the end, then, he too has his metaphysics and his theory as to what its structure and composition ultimately must be. If Nihilism depends in any logical way upon this view, then Nihilism is false or, if it is true, it entails the falsity of its own presuppositions and cannot be seriously asserted. (Danto, *Nietzsche as Philosopher*, expanded ed. [New York: Columbia University Press, 2005], 62.)

This charge is characteristic of many analytical readings of Nietzsche.

[19] There may simply be a contradiction between early and late Nietzsche on this point, rather than a shift in emphasis and terminology as he came to reject Schopenhauer's pessimism. By 1886, at least, he was clearly less interested in metaphysical comfort, advocating instead, a radical affirmation of life in the face of suffering. See Tyler T. Roberts, *Contesting Spirit: Nietzsche, Affirmation, Religion* (Princeton, NJ: Princeton University Press, 1998), chap. 1.

[20] Plato, *Phaedrus*, trans. Benjamin Jowett, 247.

[21] *HH*, "The Wanderer and His Shadow," 1.

[22] See Maudemarie Clark, *Nietzsche on Truth and Philosophy* (Cambridge: Cambridge University Press, 1990), esp. chap. 3. Still, in later unpublished notes, he abandons the Kantian thesis: "That things possess a constitution in themselves quite apart from interpretation and subjectivity, is a quite idle hypothesis" (*WP*, 560). The hypothesis needs to be *idle* rather than *false* because it cannot be verified, shown to be either true or false. Put differently, Kant "no longer has a right to his distinction" (*WP*, 553).

Notes

[23] Indeed, modernity's less radical critics of the Enlightenment were likewise unable to bear the dismissal of secular reason when it dismissed God. Merold Westphal names Marx and Freud among these (Westphal, *Suspicion and Faith: The Religious Uses of Modern Atheism* [Grand Rapids: Eerdmans, 1993, 227).

[24] *D*, 129.

[25] *BGE*, 32.

[26] See *GM*, preface, 2–3.

[27] *D*, 95.

[28] *Ibid.* In an early dismissal of Christianity (*HH*, 113), Nietzsche makes two kinds of accusations: that there is no proof that Jesus is the son of God and that Christian belief is absurd by modern standards ("Can one believe that things of this sort are still believed in?").That there is lack of proof is not meant to be devastating (it need not be for Nietzsche) except that Christian Europe tended to demand proof of everything else, indicating that Christianity could not help but exist as a distortion of the original insofar as modern Christians fail to see how un-modern their religion really is. He notes that the cross is used "in an age which no longer knows the meaning and shame of the cross." I confess to finding this last point thoroughly sibylline.

[29] *A*, 47.

[30] See *GS*, 125.

[31] Karl Barth, *The Epistle to the Romans*, trans. Edwyn C. Hoskyns (Oxford: Oxford University Press, 1968), 238.

[32] Hans Urs von Balthasar, *The Theology of Karl Barth*, trans. Edward T. Oakes, S.J. (San Francisco, CA: Ignatius, 1992), 68.

[33] See Rüdiger Safranski, *Nietzsche: A Philosophical Biography*, trans. Shelley Frisch (London: Granta, 2002), 79.

[34] Nietzsche may have come to regret his lack of offering proofs, something suggested by his 1886 preface to *BT* in which he chastises his first book for being suspicious of "the very notion of proof, being a book written for initiates, a 'music' for men christened in the name of music and held together by special esthetic experiences, a shibboleth for the highbrow confraternity" ("A Critical Backward Glance," 3).

[35] I am not persuaded by Arthur Danto that the books from Nietzsche's middle period are near random collections of aphorisms that bear no resemblance to each other nor presuppose knowledge of each other (*Nietzsche as Philosopher*, chap. 1). It may be that they connect in less obvious ways—existentially rather than literarily. Safranski speaks of a "long logic" that connects the aphorisms, organizing them intentionally so that "anyone on the lookout for their central arguments would almost inevitably fall flat on his face" (*Nietzsche*, 234).

[36] *HH*, "Mixed Opinions and Maxims," 129. Cited from *The Portable Nietzsche*, ed. and trans. by Walter Kaufmann (London:Viking Penguin, 1968), 65.

[37] *HH*, I, 2.

[38] This is because every reader is an interpreter and therefore a creator of meaning (*WP*, 767).

[39] But this did not prevent Nietzsche from being playful with personal allusions in his texts. Danto notes that "one would have had to be privy to much of his

biography not to have taken literally what was sometimes only a pun for initiates. His great misfortune has been the literalness with which even his more sympathetic critics have interpreted him" (*Nietzsche as Philosopher*, 182).

40 *Z*, I, "On the Gift-Giving Virtue," 3. It should be pointed out that Nietzsche may have made importunate use of aphorism, as John Figgis thinks: "His style, though brilliant, has no repose, and is fatiguing to read for long. Strings of aphorisms are rarely attractive." John Neville Figgis, *The Will to Freedom* (New York: Charles Scribner's Sons, 1917), 247.

41 *GM*, Preface, 8.

42 See Rowan Williams, *The Wound of Knowledge* (Eugene, Oregon, OR: Wipf and Stock, 2000), chap. 1.

43 In particular, Nietzsche's view of Christianity was colored by German liberal Protestantism and shows very little familiarity with the breadth of the historic Christian tradition. David Bentley Hart observes that Nietzsche seems only to know about the satisfaction theory of atonement and to have taken for granted that an emphasis on moral interiority is characteristic of Christian thought in ways that far exceed the German Protestantism of his day (Hart, *The Beauty of the Infinite: The Aesthetics of Christian Truth* [Grand Rapids, MI: Eerdmans, 2003], 95 n. 98). Likewise, F. A. Lea remarks, "If Jesus of *The Antichrist* is a eunuch, it was Nietzsche who emasculated him" (*The Tragic Philosopher: Friedrich Nietzsche* [London: Athlone, 1993], 338).

44 See Kathleen Marie Higgins, *Nietzsche's Zarathustra* (Philadelphia, PA: Temple University Press, 1987), chap. 5.

45 Zarathustra's first such exhortation comes in *Z*, Prologue, 3.

46 "Like nihilism, Christianity can, should, embrace the differential flux." John Milbank, "'Postmodern Critical Augustinianism': A Short *Summa* in Forty Two Responses to Unasked Questions," in *Modern Theology* 7: 3 (April 1991): 225–237 (p. 227 cited). See Chapter 6 of the present work for further explication of this claim.

47 It is impossible to do justice to this debate here. I am only modestly trying to indicate that there is such a debate and that the sides are not necessarily described in terms that convert in an obvious way with Nietzsche's.

48 George Lindbeck, *The Nature of Doctrine* (Philadelphia, PA: Westminster, 1984).

49 *BT*, 10.

50 Nicholas Adams helpfully points out that the creeds are actually prayers rather than lists of beliefs; for instance, they end with Amen. Nicholas Adams, "Reasoning in Tradition," in *The Blackwell Companion to Christian Ethics*, ed. Stanley Hauerwas and Samuel Wells (Oxford: Blackwell, 2004), 209–221. Therefore, confessing the creed is both an affirmation and an entreaty that has the form of "I believe; help my unbelief," making it a present tense enactment.

51 Robert W. Jenson, *Systematic Theology: The Triune God*, vol. 1 (Oxford: Oxford University Press, 1997), 4–5.

52 Herbert McCabe, *God Matters* (London: Continuum, 2005), 175.

53 Zarathustra explicitly seems to invite this comparison in his telling of riddles when he declares, "He that has ears to hear, let him hear!" (*Z*, III, "On the

Vision and the Riddle," 1 paralleling Matthew 13: 9, 43, Mark 4: 9, 23, Luke 8: 8, 14: 35; see also *Z*, 1, "On the Gift-Giving Virtue," 1).

[54] Mark 4: 11–12.

[55] *A*, 47.

[56] Nietzsche's aphoristic works were written between 1878 and 1881; the parable of the madman is introduced in *GS* (1882) and is vastly expanded in *Z* (1883–1885).

[57] We might imagine a Nietzschian disdain for those who write biblical commentaries that attempt to explain parables.

[58] Hans Urs von Balthasar, *A Theology of History* (San Francisco, CA: Ignatius, 1994), 36–37.

[59] *PT*, 81.

[60] "To admit a belief merely because it is a custom—but that means to be dishonest, cowardly, lazy!" (*D*, 101).

[61] *PT*, 79.

[62] Although Nietzsche comes close to assigning this exact opposition on Christianity when he writes that "Whatever a theologian feels to be true *must* be false: this is almost a criterion of truth" (*A*, 9).

[63] *WP*, 540.

[64] See Clark, *Nietzsche on Truth and Philosophy*, 21–25.

[65] *TL*, 1, cited from *PT*.

[66] Clark, *Nietzsche on Truth and Philosophy*, 22.

[67] John Milbank critiques Nietzsche precisely for not being able to provide a disinterested myth. Milbank, *Theology and Social Theory: Beyond Secular Reason* (Oxford: Blackwell, 1990), 282.

[68] See *Z*, I, "On Reading and Writing."

[69] Figgis, *Will to Freedom*, 217.

[70] Nietzsche, of course, knew nothing of recorded music. This is important because live music can only be experienced without being consumed, whereas modern music collections can be consumed because they can be archived and cataloged. In Nietzsche's time, the equivalent to this might have been the score, but only musicians would collect scores which, even so, can only be experienced once actual music is produced. And the production of music is always a *present* experience, which is perhaps why Nietzsche later commented that *BT* was composed for a singing voice—it is meant to resist the timeless, non-involvement that would come to characterize recorded music.

[71] "The world seen from within, the world described and defined according to its 'intelligible character'—it would be 'will to power and nothing else.'" (*BGE*, 36).

[72] See *TI*, esp. Preface: "There are more idols than realities in the world."

[73] Alasdair MacIntyre, *Three Rival Versions of Moral Enquiry: Encyclopaedia, Genealogy, and Tradition* (Notre Dame: University of Notre Dame Press, 1990), 48–49.

[74] This, it will be recalled, was Clark's critique. Figgis also misunderstands this when he faults Nietzsche's genealogy of slave morality for being inaccurate and only relying on Nietzsche's force of personality to persuade: "To a mind

Notes

at all trained, his early history of the Jewish people and of early Christianity is a travesty of the facts" (*Will to Freedom*, 232). Genealogy flies below the surface of facts. Indeed, Nietzsche even admits to inventing fictions where he could not find what he needed (*HH*, Preface, 1), recalling a similar claim by Michel Foucault in a most Nietzschean spirit. See Foucault, *Power/Knowledge Selected Interviews and Other Writings 1972–1977*, ed. Colin Gordon (Harlow: Pearson Education, 1980), 193.

[75] Nietzsche's frequent association of Christianity with Platonism is an example. It is rhetorically powerful but lacks a great deal of philosophical precision.

[76] *HH*, "The Wanderer and His Shadow," 4.

[77] But then, of course, the truth of these sentences is a problem for the very reasons I am attempting to explain.

[78] *BT*, 20.

[79] Ibid.

[80] 1 Cor. 1: 23.

Chapter 3: Culture of nothingness

[1] *UM*, "On the Uses and Disadvantages of History for Life," 1.

[2] Ibid.

[3] Ibid., 10.

[4] Ibid.

[5] We may notice how speaking of skill in this way resembles the way that, for Aristotle, law inculcates virtue only to obviate law. But in both cases, this cannot be a complete disregard (of history, of law) since the very ability to transcend them nevertheless owes to them.

[6] *UM*, "On the Uses and Disadvantages of History for Life," 10.

[7] Cited in Fritz Stern, *The Politics of Cultural Despair: A Study in the Rise of the Germanic Ideology* (Berkeley, CA: University of California Press, 1961), 103.

[8] *UM*, "On the Uses and Disadvantages of History for Life," 9.

[9] And so when pressed, Nietzsche preferred that the present be lived as a function of the *future* (see *Z*, I, "On the Love of Neighbor").

[10] In addition to the opening sections of *HH*, see *TI*, "'Reason' in Philosophy."

[11] In this regard, even those Anabaptists who followed Zwingli in denying the real presence of Christ in the bread and wine nevertheless sought to discover the reality of Christ's presence in the gathered fellowship, the church. See John D. Rempel, *The Lord's Supper in Anabaptism* (Scottdale, PA: Herald Press, 1993).

[12] See Peter M. Candler, Jr., "Liturgically Trained Memory: A Reading of *Summa Theologiae* III.83," *Modern Theology* 20: 3 (July 2004). I am indebted to Candler's analysis of Aquinas in this section.

[13] I admit that this makes me wonder about the status of those who do not partake of the Eucharist but come forward for a blessing, although coming forward is itself the other half of the receipt of blessing and therefore it cannot be a one-sided transaction.

[14] 1 Cor. 11: 26.

[15] See Plato's *Phaedo* (65b) in which Socrates asks,

Notes

Is the body an obstacle when one associates it in the search for knowledge? I mean, for example, do men find any truth in sight or hearing, or are not even the poets forever telling us that we do not see or hear anything accurately, and surely if those two physical senses are not clear or precise, our other senses can hardly be accurate, as they are all inferior to these. Do you not think so? (*Plato: Five Dialogues*, trans. G. M. A. Grube [Indianapolis, IN: Hackett, 1981], 101.)

As Nietzsche knew, this is not just an epistemology, but is part of a much larger dualistic metaphysics of body and soul. From among many examples in Plato, see *Timaeus* (41Df) according to which all souls were created identical and only become individuated when they take on bodies and, even then, only temporarily. Yearning after disembodied (and as such, unhistorical) knowledge is just the yearning of the soul for its original condition.

[16] *TI*, "'Reason' in Philosophy," 1.

[17] *WP*, 567.

[18] Descartes, *Objections and Replies*, 443 cited from *Descartes: Selected Philosophical Writings*, trans. John Cottingham, Robert Stoothoff, Dugald Murdoch (Cambridge: Cambridge University Press, 1988), 149.

[19] *TI*, "'Reason' in Philosophy," 2.

[20] Ibid.

[21] Ibid., 5.

[22] For example, the linguistic philosophy of Wittgenstein comes to mind. And, though it may not be the most sophisticated illustration of the trend, George Lakoff and Mark Johnson's *Philosophy in the Flesh: The Embodied Mind and its Challenge to Western Thought* (New York: Basic Books, 1999) is certainly emblematic.

[23] See Edward Schillebeeckx, *The Eucharist* (New York: Burns & Oates, 2005).

[24] Hans Urs von Balthasar points out how, in addition to being sensual for the one who partakes, the Eucharist is also sensual for Christ himself; it involves his whole bodily reality. See his *A Theology of History* (San Francisco: Ignatius, 1994), 97.

[25] One then wonders whether it undervalues the Eucharist as an incarnation of Christ, exactly the notion a sensualist doctrine intends to uphold.

[26] This also owes to another respect in which Aristotle's metaphysics of body and soul differs from Plato's. For Plato, body and soul can be imagined as existing independently (at least the soul existing apart from the body). But for Aristotle, the soul is the *form of the body* (as it also is for Thomas Aquinas; see *Summa Theologiae*, I.75.5): no body can exist without form since we would not call it a body just as it makes no sense to talk about form on its own—form *of what*?

[27] *EH*, "Thus Spoke Zarathustra," 4.

[28] I am indebted to the unpublished work of Jonathan Tran on this topic.

[29] See Rüdiger Safranski, *Nietzsche: A Philosophical Biography*, trans. Shelley Frisch (London: Granta, 2002), 117.

30 Examples of this are exceedingly numerous. A recent example is Sharon D. Welch, a self-proclaimed post-Christian who in *After Empire: The Art and Ethos of Enduring Peace* (Minneapolis, MN: Augsburg Fortress, 2004) wants "justice without transcendence" (23). Nietzsche would have been, and was, enraged by this—if you are going to be post-Christian, have the courage really to be it.

31 *WP*, 1054.

32 According to Safranski (*Nietzsche*, 123), Nietzsche despised the way that Eduard von Hartmann found contentment in the progress of history.

33 Safranski's exposition of Hegel is very useful (ibid., 120–121).

34 *UM*, "On the Uses and Disadvantages of History for Life," 8.

35 Ibid., 1.

36 Miroslav Volf, *The End of Memory: Remembering Rightly in a Violent World* (Grand Rapids, MI: Eerdmans, 2006), 163.

Chapter 4: Un-meaning history

1 Nietzsche referred to *Z* as "the most decisive work there is" (Letter of Nov. 22, 1888, cited in Rüdiger Safranski, *Nietzsche: A Philosophical Biography*, trans. Shelley Frisch [London: Granta, 2002], 370).

2 *GS*, 341.

3 This plan for this volume is found in *WP*, 1057.

4 I take this to mean that, so long as Nietzsche wants the Eternal Recurrence to have a propositional character that may be buttressed by scientific proof, he falls into contradiction.

5 *EH*, "Thus Spoke Zarathustra," 1.

6 *WP*, 1063.

7 See *Z*, III, "On the Vision and the Riddle," 2.

8 Ibid., 1.

9 Ibid., 2.

10 *EH*, Foreword, sec. 3.

11 *GS*, 276; cf. *WP*, 1041. Nietzsche continued to use this phrase until he stopped writing.

12 "If the world had a goal, it must have been reached," (*WP*, 1062).

13 Ibid., 1066.

14 Ibid., 1065.

15 *EH*, "Why I Am So Clever," 10.

16 Safranski thinks Nietzsche contradicts himself on this point (*Nietzsche*, chap. 10).

17 *TI*, "Maxims and Arrows," 12.

18 *BGE*, 228. In these remarks, one wonders if Nietzsche is accusing the utilitarians of being unconsciously Kantian.

19 Ibid.

20 *Z*, Prologue, 5.

21 Ibid., 4.

22 *Z*, III, "On Old and New Tablets," 27.

23 Josef Pieper, *The End of Time: A Meditation on the Philosophy of History*, trans. Michael Bullock (San Francisco, CA: Ignatius, 1999), 61.

Notes

[24] Abraham Joshua Heschel, *The Sabbath* (New York: Farrar, Straus and Giroux, 2005).

[25] But rest can be a proper cessation of action for us *because* it is not cessation for God since otherwise our ceasing to act would be our ceasing to exist. But this is only a way of saying that God is awake while we sleep.

[26] Pseudo-Dionysius posited a different priority of existence to God's essence, namely, goodness. On this account, which differs from the main account represented by Aquinas, God's goodness elicits the desire of all things, including those things that do not exist. Non-being, therefore, would not on this account be morally neutral but, in fact, good to the extent that even those things that do not exist desire God even while they do not desire existence since, in so desiring, they are in fact desiring what is more fundamental to God's essence. See Jean-Luc Marion, *God without Being: Hors Texte*, trans. Thomas A. Carlson (Chicago, IL: University of Chicago Press, 1991), 73–83. Nietzsche's reflections on the will might well be in sympathy with those (non) things that only "exist" as desire but have no essence since the will, likewise, can never be an essence as such. Even so, the desire of all things, for Pseudo-Dionysius, makes of God its final cause and would likely make Nietzsche suspicious of the attendant teleology.

[27] *Z*, I, "On the Adder's Bite."

[28] *Z*, Prologue, 5.

[29] Ibid., 9.

[30] See F. A. Lea, *The Tragic Philosopher: Friedrich Nietzsche* (London: Athlone, 1993), 203.

[31] *WP*, 692.

[32] Bernard Reginster's account of the will to power brings a lot of clarity to a bewildering concept. See Reginster, *The Affirmation of Life: Nietzsche on Overcoming Nihilism* (Cambridge, MA: Harvard University Press, 2006), chap. 3.

[33] *GS*, 363.

[34] *Z*, I, "On War and Warriors."

[35] Still, Nietzsche never took steps specifically to repudiate his degrees as did his contemporary, Julius Langbehn, who wrote to the University of Munich asking them to remove his name from their list of graduates: "It is my intention . . . to divest myself of the title of doctor." When the University did not comply, Langbehn took matters into his own hands, tearing up his diploma and mailing it to them. See Stern, *Politics of Cultural Despair*, 102. Langbehn was an insufferable megalomaniac and acted on impulses that very often were Nietzschean.

[36] Isaiah 5: 13.

[37] *WP*, Preface, 3, 15.

[38] Richard Schacht defends Nietzsche against others like Danto who argue that Nietzsche is a nihilist. See Schacht *Making Sense of Nietzsche: Reflections Timely and Untimely* (Champaign, IL: University of Illinois Press, 1995), chap. 2.

[39] See Reginster, *Affirmation of Life*, chap. 1.

[40] *GM*, II, 24.

[41] Even so, Nietzsche's own pronouncement of God's death *is* partially a lament for reasons I discuss in Chapter 6.

Notes

Chapter 5: Un-powering the good

1 The Bross Lectures at Lake Forest College in Illinois published as John Neville Figgis, *The Will to Freedom* (New York: Charles Scribner's Sons, 1917).

2 Figgis, *Will to Freedom*, 266.

3 Fritz Stern, *The Politics of Cultural Despair: A Study in the Rise of the Germanic Ideology* (Berkeley: University of California Press, 1961).

4 Related is Benedict Anderson's well-known work, *Imagined Communities: Reflections on the Origin and Spread of Nationalism* (London: Verso, 1983).

5 *Z*, I, "On the New Idol."

6 Thomas Aquinas, *On Kingship*, Book 2. See *From Irenaeus to Grotius: A Sourcebook in Christian Political Thought*, ed. Oliver O'Donovan and Joan Lockwood O'Donovan (Grand Rapids, MI: Eerdmans, 1999), 335–341.

7 In this respect, Nietzsche's antipathy toward virtue is nearly identical to his antipathy toward truth.

8 Nietzsche explicitly saw the church as a kind of state (*Z*, II, "On Great Events").

9 Aquinas, *On Kingship*, 1265–1266.

10 *Z*, I, "On the New Idol."

11 *EH*, "Why I am So Wise," 3.

12 Peter Bergmann, *Nietzsche, the "Last Antipolitical German"* (Bloomington, IN: Indiana University Press, 1987).

13 See Seth Taylor, *Left-Wing Nietzscheans: The Politics of German Expressionism, 1910–1920* (New York: de Gruyter, 1990), 208–209.

14 The hermit (the "saint") asks Zarathustra, "What do you bring us as a gift?" Zarathustra does not answer because what he bears, the message of the *Übermensch*, cannot be received by one who still praises God (*Z*, Prologue, 2).

15 *Z*, I, "On the New Idol."

16 *EH*, "Why I Write Such Good Books," 1.

17 F. A. Lea, *The Tragic Philosopher: Friedrich Nietzsche* (London: Athlone, 1993), 290.

18 *Z*, I, "On the New Idol." We already know that music, for Nietzsche, is the ultimate expression of the Dionysian aspect of human life. If the people of the *Übermensch* begin to sing a song never before sung, then presumably the end of the state coincides with the destruction, or at least subordination, of the Apollonian.

19 "I do not like at all about that Jesus of Nazareth or his apostle Paul that they put so many ideas into the heads of little people, as if their modest virtues were of any consequence. We have had to pay too dearly for it: for they have brought the more valuable qualities of virtue and man into ill repute . . . ." (*WP*, 205)

20 One problem with this account is that it is perhaps much more radical than we are comfortable with. Or possibly it strikes us as much more radical than Aquinas thought it was or intended for it to be. It is certain that Aquinas could envision a tyrannical king, but he seemed to have a harder time understanding what a secular king would be. We seem to be led to an overly-simply conclusion: all non-Christian kings must be tyrants. This would mean Christians are

subject to them but not finally required to obey them. (The one who disobeys is still subject to punishment.)

[21] *A*, 2.

[22] *Z*, I, "On the Thousand and One Goals."

[23] *BGE*, 186.

[24] *GM*, "First Essay".

[25] See Alasdair MacIntyre, *After Virtue*, 3rd. ed. (Notre Dame: University of Notre Dame Press, 2007), esp. chap 5.

[26] This is essentially MacIntyre's diagnosis of the modern confusion in moral theory, though the element of self-deception is clearly Nietzschean.

[27] When specified, Nietzsche's targets in this regard were almost always the "English moralists," by which he means utilitarians. MacIntyre argues that Kant is more complicated and at one point recognized that teleology is a necessary presupposition to any morality.

> Kant was right; morality did in the eighteenth century, as a matter of historical fact, presuppose something very like the teleological scheme of God, freedom and happiness as the final crown of virtue which Kant propounds. Detach morality from that framework and you will no longer have morality; or, at the very least, you will have radically transformed its character. (MacIntyre, *After Virtue*, 56)

[28] *BGE*, 5.

[29] It may therefore be a mark of honesty that Nietzsche called himself a psychologist despite where psychology falls (lower down) in the hierarchy of the sciences, which was the case as much in the nineteenth century as now.

[30] See *D*, 189.

[31] *Z*, I, "On the Adder's Bite."

[32] As Merold Westphal observes in *Suspicion and Faith: The Religious Uses of Modern Atheism* (Grand Rapids: Eerdmans, 1993), 233.

[33] *Z*, I, "On the Flies of the Market Place."

[34] Foucault made this attempt at the very end of his career in a series of lectures, some of which were posthumously published from an audio transcript as Michel Foucault, *Fearless Speech*, ed. Joseph Pearson (Los Angeles: Semiotext(e), 2001).

[35] *Z*, I, "On the Way of the Creator."

[36] Charles Taylor, *Philosophy and the Human Sciences, Philosophical Papers 2* (Cambridge: Cambridge University Press, 1985), 211–229.

[37] *BGE*, 164.

[38] Cited in Lea, *The Tragic Philosopher*, 338.

[39] *Z*, I, "On the New Idol." This leads to the observation that Nietzsche should rightly be thought of as an ascetic thinker. See, for example (following Walter Kaufmann) Tyler T. Roberts, *Contesting Spirit: Nietzsche, Affirmation, Religion* (Princeton, NJ: Princeton University Press, 1998), chap. 3. As a simple nomad for many of his mature years, Nietzsche's own life attests to this claim.

[40] See Westphal, *Suspicion and Faith*, 233. At the popular level, the theology of Dan Brown's novels is intensely non-Augustinian in this regard. For Brown, the universe achieves harmony through balancing good and evil forces just as good and evil are only definable against each other. Christianity may join with Nietzsche in condemning this kind of metaphysics in which there is *only* reaction.

[41] In this respect, Nietzsche might protest that the Augustinian doctrine is an attempt to "solve" evil and, as such, cannot help but justify its existence even while denying it positive existence. But Augustine does not justify evil, only goodness and freedom.

[42] John Howard Yoder, "Are the Tyrants Really in Charge? Realism and Radical Change" (unpublished).

[43] John Howard Yoder, *The Royal Priesthood: Essays Ecclesiological and Ecumenical*, ed. Michael G. Cartwright (Scottdale, PA: Herald, 1998), 251.

[44] Yoder associated being truthful with acknowledging human fallibility. "Any existing church is not only fallible but in fact peccable. That is why there needs to be a constant potential for reformation and in the more dramatic situations a readiness for the reformation to be 'radical'." John Howard Yoder, *The Priestly Kingdom: Social Ethics as Gospel* (Notre Dame: University of Notre Dame Press, 1984), 5.

[45] Yoder saw this as part of bearing a truthful witness:

> the continuing pertinence of the historical memory of Jesus, via the New Testament, as a lever for continuing critique, is part of the message itself. The capacity for, or in fact the demand for, self-critique is part of what must be shared with people of other faiths and ideologies. (Yoder, *Royal Priesthood*, 251)

Chapter 6: Dispelling being

[1] See Michel Haar, "Nietzsche and the Metamorphosis of the Divine," trans. M. Gendre in *Post-Secular Philosophy*, ed. Phillip Blond (London: Routledge, 1998), 157–176.

[2] *GS*, 125, cited from *The Portable Nietzsche*, ed. and trans. by Walter Kaufmann (London: Viking Penguin, 1968), 95.

[3] In other words, Nietzsche never tried to prove the claims of naturalism that left no room for God the life-giver and even though he presupposed the truth of naturalism in this regard, he was not driven by it. If he had been, he would have been too much a scientist captivated by facts (scientific laws and theorems to explain phenomena which formerly had been explained by God), something he refused to be on other grounds.

[4] *TI*, "How the 'True World' Finally Became a Fable."

[5] Ibid.

[6] Ibid.

[7] For this idea, I am indebted in this section to Robert W. Jenson, *Systematic Theology: The Triune God*, vol. 1 (Oxford: Oxford University Press, 1997), chap. 13, esp. p. 214.

Notes

8 See, for example, Paul J. Griffiths, "The Very Idea of Religion," *First Things*, 103 (May 2000): 30–35. The works of Talal Asad and Jonathan Z. Smith are seminal, as is Timothy Fitzgerald's *The Ideology of Religious Studies* (Oxford: Oxford University Press, 2000).

9 Jean-Luc Marion, *God Without Being: Hors Texte*, trans. Thomas A. Carlson (Chicago, IL: University of Chicago Press, 1991), esp. 38.

10 Cited in Marion, *God Without Being*, 35.

11 Robert W. Jenson, *Systematic Theology: The Works of God*, vol. 2 (Oxford: Oxford University Press, 1999), 214.

12 Jer. 10: 4–5.

13 Rowan Williams, *Grace and Necessity: Reflections on Art and Love* (London: Continuum, 2005), 26, 29.

14 Marion, *God without Being*, 24.

15 2 Cor. 3: 18.

16 Letter of October 22, 1888, cited in Rüdiger Safranski, *Nietzsche: A Philosophical Biography*, trans. Shelley Frisch (London: Granta, 2002), 369.

17 John Milbank, *Theology and Social Theory* (Oxford: Blackwell, 1990), esp. 278.

18 John Milbank, "'Postmodern Critical Augustinianism': A Short Summa in Forty-two Responses to Unasked Questions, " *Modern Theology* 7:3 (April 1991): 225–237 (esp. 227).

19 I have in mind Romand Coles and William Connolly.

20 This is why even though it is through reason that the "true world" came to be thought of as unattainable, it is not finally expunged through reason, but through the will, which is to say that in the absence of such willing, reason may still submit to religious fantasies. This alone is enough to make Nietzsche a severe critic of the Enlightenment.

21 I have in mind the recent, remarkable book by Jonathan Lear, *Radical Hope: Ethics in the Face of Cultural Devastation* (Cambridge, MA: Harvard University Press, 2006) in which he demonstrates the level of incommensurability between a Native American tribe and the moral and legal (and otherwise) expectations of the US government once the tribe was moved to a reservation.

22 William Connolly, "Suffering, Justice, and the Politics of Becoming" in *Moral Spaces: Rethinking Ethics and World Politics*, ed. David Campbell and Michael J. Shapiro (Minneapolis, MN: University of Minnesota Press, 1999), esp. 132.

23 *WP*, 511.

24 Sheldon S. Wolin makes this point when he argues for "fugitive democracy" in *Politics and Vision: Continuity and Innovation in Western Political Thought*, Expanded ed. (Princeton, NJ: Princeton University Press, 2004), chap. 14. Wolin, it should be noted, has in mind American democracy where there is a paradox: "while democracy is widely proclaimed as the political identity of the American system, the demos is becoming disenchanted with the form that claims it" (ibid., 601).

25 William Connolly, *Politics and Ambiguity* (Madison, WI: University of Wisconsin Press, 1987), 11.

26 Michael Sandel is a self-proclaimed communitarian of this sort and John Rawls has turned into a caricature of himself as a liberal champion of individual rights.

[27] *GS*, 344.

[28] Ibid.

[29] *GM*, III, 27.

[30] Ibid.

[31] Or more accurately, perhaps, the will to truth is only a guise of the will to power. As life itself tells Zarathustra, "verily, my will to power walks also on the heels of your will to truth" (*Z*, II, "On Self-Overcoming").

[32] Gilles Deleuze, *Foucault*, trans. Séan Hand (London: Athlone, 1988), 25.

[33] *Z*, I, "On Reading and Writing."

[34] Yet this should not be taken to imply that Nietzsche thought that the course of one's life is always loveable in its continuance; suicide may in fact affirm life in a way that living out an old age may not (*HH*, I.80). When one lacks the strength any longer to be able to attain life's goals, suicide is, for Nietzsche, a noble act whereas he thinks that the ways that religions generally do not affirm it is a form of *ressentiment*—a resignation of the will to power—whereby they disguise their actual denial of life with an affirmation.

[35] Ibid.

[36] Job 10:1.

[37] Job 42:3.

[38] Job 1:9.

[39] *Gregory of Nyssa: The Life of Moses*, ed. and trans. Abraham Malherbe and Everett Ferguson, Classics of Western Spirituality (New York: Paulist, 1978).

[40] Ibid., II, 252.

[41] *Z*, II, "On Self-Overcoming."

[42] *Gregory of Nyssa: The Life of Moses*, II, 239.

[43] Safranski, *Nietzsche*, 278.

[44] This last equation is an assumption I am making, even though I strongly suspect that the will to love is also a kind of love, at least in respect of the manner in which it is satisfied only in its continual exercise.

[45] *Hexaemeron*, i.3.

Chapter 7: Dancing and singing

[1] *GM*, First Essay, 7.

[2] Cited in Rüdiger Safranski, *Nietzsche: A Philosophical Biography*, trans. Shelley Frisch (London: Granta, 2002),, 371.

[3] *Z*, I, "On Reading and Writing."

[4] Letter of January 21, 1887, cited in Safranski, *Nietzsche*, 368.

[5] *NCW*, "Where I Offer Objections."

[6] *NCW*, "Wagner as a Danger," 1.

[7] Ibid.

[8] Here if Nietzsche himself seems to offer the kind of critique I made of him in Chapter 6, it is important to remember that Nietzsche is not opposed to Wagner's metaphysics, but that chaos names a reality that is only staged for effect such that, even though it may resemble the Dionysian in some respects, it is really nothing more than an instrumentalized performance.

[9] *NCW*, "We Antipodes."

Notes

[10] Ibid.

[11] Nietzsche had earlier praised Wagner over against Goethe on fairly similar terms:

> It is true that such a nature as Goethe's has and gives more enjoyment, something mild and nobly prodigal hovers about it, whereas the violence of Wagner's current may terrify and scare one away from the sight of a hero who, even in regard to modern culture, "has not learned fear". (*UM*, "Richard Wagner in Bayreuth," 3)

Perhaps Nietzsche came to conclude that Wagner's violence itself masked a more fundamental fear, particularly as Wagner's popularity grew beyond what Nietzsche, at first, must have thought possible within modern culture.

[12] *TI*, "Maxims and Arrows," 33. I am here relying on Safranski, *Nietzsche*, 344–345.

[13] *Z*, I, "The Dancing Song."

[14] Ibid.

[15] *Z*, I, "The Tomb Song."

[16] *Z*, III, "The Other Dancing Song."

[17] *Z*, I, "The Tomb Song."

[18] Edwin Dodge Hardin, "Nietzsche's Service to Christianity," *The American Journal of Theology* 18: 4 (Oct. 1914): 548–549.

Index

Index

Index

the Fall, 103

falsehood, 5, 38, 73, 108, 125, 137, 152n22, 155n62

fate, 74, 82; *See also amor fati*

fideism, 73

Figgis, John Neville, 92–93, 154n40, 155n74

fire, 24–25, 27

Fitzgerald, Timothy, 163n8

flux, 23, 25, 27, 34, 74, 125–127, 130, 133, 152n18, 154n46

forgetting, 38, 48, 51–53, 63, 65–68, 83

forgiveness, 11, 66–68, 109, 115

Foucault, Michel, 12, 29, 95, 110, 126, 130–131, 135, 156n74, 161n34

freedom, 62–63, 89, 110–112

French Revolution, 65

Freud, Sigmund, 153n23

friendship, 79, 138
with God, 96, 100, 103

fugitive democracy, 131, 163n24

genealogy, 29–30, 41–42, 82, 105, 109–110, 112, 117, 140, 155n74

Germany, 28, 43, 66, 93

gift, 3, 10, 54, 68, 127, 160n14

Gnostic/gnosticism, 9, 22

Goethe, Johann Wolfgang von, 146, 165n11

Greece, 14, 22, 43, 59, 110

Gregory of Nyssa, 140–141

Griffiths, Paul J., 163n8

Haar, Michel, 162n1

happiness, 52, 77–78, 80, 161n27

Hardin, Edwin Dodge, 165n18

Hart, David Bentley, 151n15, 154n43

Hartmann, Eduard von, 158n32

Hegel, Georg W. F., 12, 62, 65–66, 125

Heidegger, Martin, 121

Heller, Erich, 150n11

Heraclitus, 49, 58

Heschel, Abraham, 81

Higgins, Kathleen Marie, 154n44

historicism, 63, 65

history, 8, 23, 25, 27, 32, 33, 34, 35, 45–51, 54, 55–57, 60–65, 71–72, 77, 90, 101, 110, 125, 139, 142, 156n5, 158n32

Holy Spirit, 8–9, 34

Homer, 24, 110

Horkheimer, Max, 146

human nature, 66, 107–108

Hume, David, 106

humility, 26, 38, 137

icon, 123–124

iconoclasm, 121

idol/idolatry, 2, 8, 30, 42, 52, 59, 88, 90–91, 94–96, 98, 104, 117–120, 122–123, 131, 141–143

Iliad, 24

impermanence, 25, 27, 58

India, 43, 59

individual, 21–22, 49, 62, 79–80, 100, 102, 133, 151n8, 163n26

information, 20, 36–37, 72, 134

injustice, 23, 66, 95, 103, 110

interpretation, 9, 29, 41, 50, 152n22

intuitions, 41

Isaiah, 87

Israel, 9

Jenson, Robert W., 35, 122, 150n9, 162n7

Index

violence, 6, 21, 90, 113–114,
126–129, 165n11; *see also*
non-violence
virtue, 24, 32, 80, 84, 95–98,
102–103, 109, 127, 156n5,
160nn7, 19, 161n27
Volf, Miroslav, 67

Wagner, Richard, 14, 16, 47, 49,
64, 145–146, 164n8,
165n11
Welch, Sharon D., 158n30
Wolin, Sheldon, 131, 163n24
Westphal, Merold, 11, 153n23
will to power, 42, 66, 85–86, 89,
104, 111, 120, 134–138,
141–142, 147, 152n18,
155n71, 159n32, 164nn31, 34
will to love, *see* love

will to truth, 14, 110, 134–137,
142, 164n31
Williams, Rowan, 122
Williams, Stephen N., 151n15
winter doctrines, 130, 133
wisdom, 146–148
Dionysian, 31, 42
witness (Christian), 9, 10, 115,
118, 162n45
Wittgenstein, Ludwig, 78,
150n11, 157n22
worship, 2, 7, 34, 54–56, 67,
97–98, 124, 140, 150n7

Yoder, John Howard, 113–114,
162nn42, 44, 45
Young, Julian, 150n12

Zwingli, Ulrich, 156n11